THE VIRTUE

OF

RESILIENCE

THE VIRTUE
OF
RESILIENCE

JAMES D. WHITEHEAD
and
EVELYN EATON WHITEHEAD

ORBIS  BOOKS
Maryknoll, New York 10545

ORBIS BOOKS
Maryknoll, New York 10545

Fathers and Brothers
MARYKNOLL™

Founded in 1970, Orbis Books endeavors to publish works that enlighten the mind, nourish the spirit, and challenge the conscience. The publishing arm of the Maryknoll Fathers and Brothers, Orbis seeks to explore the global dimensions of the Christian faith and mission, to invite dialogue with diverse cultures and religious traditions, and to serve the cause of reconciliation and peace. The books published reflect the views of their authors and do not represent the official position of the Maryknoll Society. To learn more about Maryknoll and Orbis Books, please visit our website at www.maryknollsociety.org.

Manufactured in the United States of America

Library of Congress Cataloging-in-Publication Data

Whitehead, James D.
   The virtue of resilience / James D. Whitehead and Evelyn Eaton Whitehead.
      pages cm
   Includes bibliographical references.
   ISBN 978-1-62698-160-7 (pbk.)
   1. Christian life. 2. Resilience (Personality trait)—Religious aspects—Christianity. I. Title.
   BV4509.5.W46 2016
   248.8'6—dc23

                                                      2015020706

Contents

Chapter One
The Grace of Resilience
Recruiting, Reframing, Resolving

Chapter Two
Personal Resilience—The Role of the Emotions
The Interplay of Fear, Courage, and Patience

Chapter Three
Resilience and the Faces of Power
Personal Power as a Foundation of Resilience

Chapter Four
Social Resilience—Crisis and Adaptability
Holding Environments—Loyalty and Flexibility

Chapter Five
Spiritual Resilience—The Transformation of Adversity
Resources of Belonging and Resistance

Chapter Six
A Soldier's Resilience—Strength and Vulnerability
Healing Wounds, Building Resilience

Chapter Seven
Civic Resilience—Cultivating Political Emotions
Civic Compassion—Boston and New Orleans

Chapter Eight
Resilience in Suffering
Trauma and Tragedy—Healing without Cure

Chapter Nine
Resilience at Risk—The Challenge of Integrity
The Perils of Belonging and the Virtue of Integrity

Chapter Ten
Developing Resilience—Mindfulness and Humor
Redeeming the Time and the Practice of Humor

Chapter Eleven
Practicing Resilience—Hope and Gratitude
Resources of Hope and Gratitude

Chapter Twelve
Resilience in Aging
Supporting Lifelong Resilience

Prologue

The human capacity of resilience allows us to rally our psychological and spiritual resources to withstand crises, weather repeated difficulties, and survive adversity. We might describe resilience as the immune system of the human spirit.

Personal resilience arises in a mix of loyalty and flexibility. We survive by recruiting companions, reframing our troubles, and resolving to endure. And resilience is more than an individual attribute. We labor to cultivate this capacity in our families and in civic and faith communities. In the chapters ahead we trace the strengths that come together to grace our lives with the virtue of resilience.

Chapter One

The Grace of Resilience
Recruiting, Reframing, Resolving

Suffering produces endurance, and endurance produces character, and character produces hope.

—Paul's Letter to the Romans 5:3

Resilience is a resource both obvious and mysterious. We are amazed when an athlete recovers quickly from a severe knee injury and, returning to play, then performs at an even higher level. Even more striking, the South African statesman Nelson Mandela not only survived his twenty-seven years' imprisonment as a political rebel, but he emerged with the moral integrity and spiritual strength to provide national leadership to his embattled country at a critical point in its history. What personal quality or moral strength enables such a remarkable response? The American Psychological Association identifies *resilience* as the underlying resource at play in these examples and offers this basic description: "Resilience is the process of adapting well in the face of adversity, trauma, tragedy, threats. . . . It means 'bouncing back' from difficult experiences." And resilience is a resource that can be displayed by both individuals and groups.

A gathering of dispirited disciples came together in an upper room (Acts 2). Now more than a month since Jesus' death, some in their community had reported seeing him. But these glimpses were brief and shadowy. On this day his absence weighed heavily on the group. The hope that Jesus' life had generated had evaporated. His dream of a new way of life, shaped by mercy and justice, seemed defeated.

In the scriptural account that Christians read on the feast of Pentecost, the record of what happened next is presented in mythic metaphors. A gust of wind moves through the room; a wisp of fire appears over each person present. In the midst of their befuddlement, they feel the stirring of hope. Surely the ideals to which Jesus' life and death had given witness were not completely lost. Unlikely gathering that they were, the disciples left this room eager to announce the truth they had received. And they did so with such energy that even those who did not speak their language received this "good news." Pentecost is for the Church the central feast of resilience.

The Three Rs of Resilience

Psychologists today insist that resilience is not a gift reserved for a select few. We meet in the human spirit the capacity to recover from grievous wounds and rally from painful setbacks. We discover, to our repeated amazement, a capacity to heal and grow yet stronger. Resilience appears early, in the charming visage of the newborn child. Parents, friends, and other caregivers gather round to celebrate this new arrival, obviously the most beautiful baby yet. The infant's smile and murmurs arouse our amazement and recruit our devotion. How can we not lavish attention and concern upon this beloved child? Unconsciously but effectively the infant recruits our care, the engaged concern that will ensure this child's survival.

The psychologist Robert Kegan judges that "the capacity to recruit another's invested regard, so uniform at birth, becomes a more varied affair as people grow older. Some people have a much greater ability to recruit people's attention to them than other people do." Without the attentive presence of others, human life is a lonely and even dangerous venture. Without this ability of recruiting others' care, personal resilience is unlikely to develop. *Recruitability*—the capacity to forge vital and enduring bonds with others—is the first "R" of resilience.

Reframing is the second factor. Faced with the hard facts of injury or insult or loss, we can refuse to be defined by these painful events. We have the ability to cast the movement of our lives in a new light, viewing the past through an alternate lens. Perhaps abuse and neglect are not the full story. Other memories may be evoked—recollections of generous care and attentive concern. Here resilience helps us reinterpret negative experiences. Without this capacity to reframe our history of personal pain, resilience has difficulty taking root.

The third "R" of resilience is *resolve*. Crucial here is the witness of those who have suffered grievous injuries and yet continue to manifest courage and grit. Nelson Mandela left his years in prison determined to contribute to his young nation's emergence in freedom. Malala Yousafzai, a Pakistani girl, survived an assassination attempt and became even more resolved in her crusade for the education of girls in her country. In these extraordinary examples, we see resilience registered as determination—the resolve to do "whatever is necessary," no matter the defeats and bruises accumulated along the way. Resolve keeps us focused on our goals, willing to resist, to fight back, to defend ideals when these are in jeopardy.

Resilience helps us tap into both personal and communal strengths. In this way we gain access to resources already existing within us (newly emerging patience and a certain self-confidence) and to resources available in our environment (the support and encouragement available from our friends and allies).

Resilience goes beyond the facile optimism that overlooks the troubles confronting us. In resilience, our response to painful experience itself becomes a constructive element. "Each negative event a person faces leads to an attempt to cope, which forces people to learn about their own capabilities, about their support networks—to learn who their real friends are" (Benedict Carey). The evidence of these real-life experiences is essential in the development of resilience.

Definitions of resilience abound. Resilience is "the ability to adapt quickly to stress without lasting mental or physical ailments" (*Oxford Handbook of Stress, Health, and Coping*). The psychologist Richard Davidson observes that "resilient people are somehow able not only to withstand but to benefit from certain kinds of stressful events and to turn adversity into advantage."

Clues to adult resilience appear already in childhood. "Inhibited or shy children are less resilient. They take longer to recover from any situation that causes them to feel stress, such as being in an unfamiliar environment or having to interact with strangers." And not surprisingly, as Richard Davidson and Sharon Begley report, "uninhibited children tend to exhibit resilience; they take such situations in stride, recovering so quickly from any initial frisson of anxiety that they barely notice it."

Psychological Resiliency

In metallurgy, resilience registers the capacity of an object to return to its original shape after being subjected to pressure. Well-tempered steel, when struck, flexes but does not break. In psychological discussion, resiliency identifies the ability to do well under stress, even over the long term.

Resilience encompasses a range of personal resources: the ability to respond effectively to difficulty, to overcome obstacles that continue to stand in the way, to find positive meaning in the midst of negative circumstances. The psychologists Janet Ramsey and Rosemary Blieszner define resilience as "the hardiness needed to change unfortunate situations into advantageous ones." They identify three ways in which psychological resiliency finds expression—recovery, resistance, reconfiguration.

Recovery focuses on the reestablishment of equilibrium; a medical example would be the gradual healing of a wound. In psychological recovery we are able to rebound from injury, to "get over" the distressing experience and return to an earlier state of well-being.

Resistance points to our ability to respond effectively to the challenges that arise in the midst of a *continuing* crisis. Here resilience is tested by how well we deal with ongoing stress as it unfolds. In these circumstances, resilience enables us to sustain a commitment to move forward, even as we recognize that difficulties may still lie ahead.

Reconfiguration helps us turn our experiences of distress and suffering into opportunities for personal growth. In the authors' view, "reconfiguration in resilient people permits them to gain control, form commitments, and challenge their own previous characteristics and beliefs." Here resilience fuels positive change and personal growth, even in the face of trauma.

Sources of Psychological Resilience

Several resources contribute to psychological resilience. Prominent here are a sense of personal effectiveness, experiences of social connectedness, and access to one's positive emotions even in the midst of distress. And many resilient adults report the significance of spirituality, expressed in their appreciation of a personal connection to the sacred.

Personal effectiveness is rooted in the conviction that determined effort will have positive results. Without this belief in personal effectiveness, experiences of trauma and disaster easily defeat us. Distracted by depression or despair, we miss opportunities to improve our situation. And with both energy and hope depleted, a sense of personal vulnerability intensifies. But supported by the success of our previous efforts to find value in difficult circumstances, we are energized to confront the difficulty currently at hand. And memories of the positive changes that have resulted from past trauma can support our efforts to confront the problems that assault us now.

Social connections provide a supportive context for our resilient response. In the face of misfortune, being part of a community expands the sense of personal efficacy: *I am not alone; we are in this together!* Collective memory holds images of both past grievances and achieved success, motivating further action now. Being part of a community helps sustain personal hopes for the future, even when progress toward positive change is slow. And community contributes to human creativity, bringing a wider range of resources into play in the face of personal difficulties or communal distress.

Deborah Khoshaba identifies three resources as crucial in developing resilience: commitment, control, challenge. Significant *commitments* shape our lives. We craft—or discover —a positive identity by staying actively connected with people who are important to us and by shaping our behavior to reflect personally chosen values. This confident awareness of "who I am" supports our resilient engagement in life.

A sense of personal mastery or *control* emerges as we take action to influence the circumstances of our life. Earlier experiences of effectiveness prompt us to confront new difficulties as these arise rather than simply give in to powerlessness and passivity. Here again, resilience is strengthened.

And when we view negative experiences as *challenges* — rather than as defeats—we are more likely to respond effectively. In difficult times, this evaluation prompts us to look to our strengths, reinforcing the conviction that we do in fact have resources to bring to bear. These resources support an awareness of personal power, transforming our stress-filled experiences into opportunities for developing resilience.

Resilience Described and Discovered

Andrew Solomon has explored the dynamics of depression in the prize-winning book *The Noonday Demon: An Atlas of Depression*. Here he explores the differences between those who are utterly defeated by a severe depression and others who manage to tap into a resilience that brings them through the suffering. "Some people suffer mild depression and are totally disabled by it; others suffer severe depression and make something of their lives anyway." And, "Some people seem to give in to their depression; others seem to battle it."

Focusing on his personal experience of severe depression, Solomon struggles to name the resources that allowed him to avoid suicide and to eventually find his way back to health. He insists that more than medicine or simple willpower were involved. "There is someone or something there stronger than chemistry or will, a *me* that got me through the revolt of myself." Acknowledging his agnosticism, Solomon searches for a name or image to capture this resilience. "I am no spiritualist and I grew up without religion, but that ropy fiber that runs through the center of me, that holds fast even when the self has been stripped away from it: anyone who lives through this knows that it is never as simple as complicated chemistry."

In his subsequent volume *Far from the Tree*, Solomon examined the experience of families caring for children born with developmental challenges, ranging from autism to Down syndrome to gender anomalies. Here too Solomon discovered children and families who flourished, even in the face of great adversity. Among the resources he discovered here was the intriguing combination of humor, hope, and resilience. "It takes a certain survivor impulse to keep going through the depression, not to cave in to it. A sense of humor is the best indicator that you will recover; it is often the best indicator that people will love you. Sustain that and you have hope."

Early in his career Solomon aspired to become a novelist. In fact, his first publication was a novel. But through his personal depression Solomon came to recognize that his central gift was as an essayist. In his subsequent—and most influential—published work Solomon has tracked the capacity for resilience in many people, but most especially in his own life. Solomon describes his struggle with depression: "I prayed to a God I had never entirely believed in, and I asked for deliverance" (*Noonday Demon*). Coming through a depression is most often experienced not as an achievement, but as a gift, a deliverance, even a grace.

Solomon shares the conviction expressed by a friend: "I had to sink so low there was nothing to believe in but God. I was slightly embarrassed to find myself drawn to religion; but it was right." Yet another colleague describes his own depression and mysterious resilience: "The fact that I got through such a catastrophic illness has permanently changed my interior landscape. I was always drawn to faith and goodness, but I wouldn't have had the drive, the moral purpose, without the breakdowns." For this person, "The most important theme in my work is redemption." Solomon concludes, "By seeing how many kinds of resilience and strength and imagination are to be found, one can appreciate not only the horror of depression but also the complexity of human vitality."

Reframing Failure

Solomon charts his own developing resilience in the subtle shifts in his relationship with his parents. As he examines the dynamics that linked them together, he began to reframe their relationship—to rename their often troubled exchanges in a kinder light. "I realized there was no refuge from my parents' meddling, I learned to value it over loneliness and call it love." In these few sentences Solomon is reframing the story of his family. He takes liberties with an earlier narrative—his "meddling parents"—renaming this engagement as genuine concern. Now the perspective has shifted and a gentler vision emerges. "I started my research aggrieved; I ended it forbearing. I set off to understand myself and ended up understanding my parents. . . . Their love always forgave me; mine came to forgive them too" (*Far from the Tree*).

Reframing seems essential to resilience: immersed in troubling situations, resilient people manage to reinterpret past experiences and even present distress. Reflecting on a chapter in their life stories, often scarred by conflict and suffering, they are able to place events within a more supportive perspective. With hope and humor they reimagine an old narrative.

The spiritual writer Henri Nouwen describes the ambiguity that lies at the core of religious faith: we experience ourselves as both blessed and broken. Often brokenness—whether failures we are responsible for or slights we have suffered—come to dominate the story, clouding our memory. But in resilience the blessings of life remains dominant. The ambiguous events of our lives may be remembered anew, now with blessing in ascendency. For Nouwen the challenge is "to pull our brokenness away from the shadow of the curse and put it under the light of blessing."

Resources

The definition of resilience by the American Psychological Association can be found in "The Road to Resilience," at www.helping.apa.org.

The Oxford Handbook of Stress, Health, and Coping, ed. Susan Folkman (New York: Oxford University Press, 2010), includes state-of-the-art essays by authors representing a range of academic perspectives.

Robert Kegan has explored the ability of the infant to recruit others' care as an essential element in human development; we quote from his discussion in *The Evolving Self* (Cambridge, MA: Harvard University Press, 1982), 116.

Richard J. Davidson and Sharon Begley discuss resilience in their *The Emotional Life of Your Brain* (New York: Penguin, 2012). The quote on inhibited children is found on page 102.

Deborah Khoshaba continues her significant contribution to the theory and practice of psychological resilience; see especially the resources she makes available online at www.HardinessInstitute.com.

Janet Ramsey and Rosemary Blieszner provide essays representing a range of perspectives in *Spiritual Resilience and Aging: Hope, Relationality, and the Creative Self* (Amityville, NY: Baywood, 2012).

See also Benedict Carey's essay "On Road to Recovery, Past Adversity Provides a Map," *New York Times* (January 4,

2011), D5.

Andrew Solomon provides valuable perspectives in *The Noonday Demon: An Atlas of Depression* (New York: Scribner, 2001) and *Far from the Tree: Parents, Children, and the Search for Identity* (New York: Scribner, 2012).

We quote from Henri Nouwen's *Life of the Beloved* (New York: Crossroad, 1993).

Chapter Two

Personal Resilience—
The Role of the Emotions

The Interplay of Fear, Courage, and Patience

We also glory in our suffering,
because we know that suffering produces perseverance.

—James 5:3

The romantic vision of resilience portrays this resource as an abiding confidence, allowing us to calmly navigate the hazards of our lives. On closer inspection, resilience is less romantic but more robust. Resilience depends on a continuing attunement to the emotions—both painful and positive—that support our vital engagement in life. Resilience allows us to harness volatile feelings, balancing fear with courage, moderating anger with patience, and calming surges of grief with the balm of gratitude.

Painful emotions—anger, fear, anxiety—help us survive. These negative feelings arise in defense of our life and dignity, sharpening our focus as we confront significant threats and dangers. Positive emotions—love, wonder, compassion—help us thrive. These arousals broaden our focus as we savor life's blessings. Painful emotions, in the service of survival, deplete our energy reserves and quickly exhaust us. Positive emotions, in service of our well-being, renew our vitality even as they give rest to our spirit.

The painful emotions of anger, fear, and guilt play an essential role in a meaningful life. But their arousals are both expensive and volatile. Expensive because they consume energy, depleting our resources and leaving us feeling exhausted. Volatile because they easily escalate into chronic moods, leading us to act in ways that make matters worse. Anger, defender of our dignity, can mushroom into chronic resentment. Fear's early warning system may spiral into a paralyzing phobia. Guilt, meant as a guardian of our goodness, can respond as a cruel judge of our every action or impulse. When these essential emotions spread beyond their proper domains, they darken our world, overshadowing our experiences of joy, delight, and appreciation. Burdened by painful emotions that have become chronic, we have little energy available for empathy or hope or even curiosity. Such a climate makes resilience difficult.

Positive feelings counteract the effects of the attention-grabbing painful emotions. The healing emotions—compassion, gratitude, joy, hope—activate the parasympathetic nervous system, lowering our heart rate and blood pressure and stimulating circulation. The psychiatrist George Vaillant distinguishes these two essential resources: "The sympathetic nervous system is catabolic: fight-or-flight uses up the body's resources. The parasympathetic nervous system is anabolic: faith, hope, and cuddling build up the body's resources." He adds, "While pain, rage, and grief provide short-term benefits, positive emotions provide benefits over the long term."

Short-term arousal and longer-term emotional balance both contribute to our resilience. So the ability to acknowledge both positive and negative emotions is crucial. And benefiting from the energy and information that each provides, we are better able to embrace the full range of our experience and to manage the stresses that arise. Offended by a friend's inconsiderate action, for example, both anger and empathy come as allies. Anger alerts us that a wrong that has been done and fuels our insistence on finding some remedy. Empathy makes us sensitive to our friend's perspective, helping us moderate our response so we don't make matters worse. Drawing on both these emotions helps us move toward a more successful resolution, one in which both our honor and our relationship remain intact.

At a deeper level, painful and positive emotions frequently arise together as we grieve a significant loss. In the midst of our sorrow over the death of someone close to us, for example, we remember our loved one's generosity and courage or recall our history of shared affection and mutual care. These cherished memories bring moments of consolation, even as we are soon overcome by a returning sense of loss. Allowing room for both sadness and gratitude is part of the strength of resilience.

Positive emotions help us rebound from experiences of psychological distress that undermine resilience. Optimism and courage, happiness and hope, pride and gratitude: these emotions ground our resilience. As John Reich and Alex Zautra observe, "Highly resilient individuals show greater morale, self-efficacy, self-reliance, perseverance and purpose in life. By summoning positive emotions, they invigorate themselves."

So psychological resilience embraces more than just *bouncing back*. Resilience opens us to positive experiences—feelings of joy, pride, curiosity, peace, vigor, affection—even in the face of adversity. These positive emotions shift our perspective, opening us to learning something new.

Most psychologists today see resilience not as a personality trait available only to a select few, but as the species-wide capacity to adapt to our changing environment. George Vaillant defines resilience as "the self-regulating tendencies within the human organism." From this perspective, resilience points to behaviors—thoughts and actions that can be learned. Through regular practice, these common tendencies can be developed into reliable resources that support personal hardiness.

A Case Study in Resilience:
Congresswoman Gabrielle Giffords

On January 8, 2011, a young man approached Gabrielle Giffords, the US Representative from Arizona, as she was speaking to a small gathering at a mall in Tucson. Without provocation or warning, he shot her in the head. Six persons in the crowd were killed, and thirteen others were wounded in this senseless attack. Giffords survived the shooting, and in an op-ed in the *New York Times* on the third anniversary of the attack she described her physical recovery and the motivation that fuels her resilience today. "Many may look at me and see mostly what I have lost. I struggle to speak, my eyesight's not great, my right arm and leg are paralyzed, and I left a job I loved representing southern Arizona in Congress."

Giffords noted that before her injury she had planned to spend the decade of her forties continuing her public service and starting a family. "I thought that by fighting for the people I cared about and loving those close to me, I could leave the world a better place. And that would be enough." Instead, she has spent the last three years learning again how to talk, how to walk, how to sign her name with her left hand. Going through the arduous therapy, she wondered, "How would I ever be able to fulfill a larger purpose?"

The gun violence in December 2012 that led to multiple deaths at the Sandy Hook school would provide Gifford an answer. "It shocked me, it motivated me, and frankly, it showed me a path." While remaining proud gun owners, she and her husband pledged to make it their mission to lobby for laws that would reduce gun violence. Her resilience is registered both in her commitment to this significant cause and her willingness to undergo the long-term therapy that will give her the strength needed to pursue this new mission.

Balancing Fear, Courage, and Patience

The world we inhabit today is truly dangerous. Adversities—setbacks, injuries, unanticipated losses—test our resilience. And these challenges elicit fear, a central resource in our repertoire of survival skills. Suicide bombers, ethnic cleansing, domestic violence, epidemic disease—there is no lack of reasons to be terrified. Even smaller everyday anxieties can unravel our plans and unsettle our lives. For some of us worry can be truly toxic, absorbing our attention so that we cannot move forward. For others, worry urges us to plan in advance: we learn that facing a challenging situation will in fact dissolve some of our concern.

Fear confronts us in many faces. But fear is not always an accurate predictor of what will bring us harm. The fears that destroy and defeat us are those that prevent our adequate response. And some of our fears are illegitimate, arising more from unresolved parts of our past than from real dangers confronting us now. An earlier defeat leaves a mark. Rather than learning from this experience, I simply become afraid. This fear leads me to protect myself in advance. When similar situations arise in the future, I *expect* to be hurt; so I wince even before I am hit.

Courage names the capacity to face our fear, without collapsing in panic or despair. Josef Pieper reminds us that the essence of courage "lies not in knowing no fear, but in not allowing oneself to be forced into evil by fear, or to be kept by fear from the realization of good." When we face a threatening task, being afraid is fitting. Courage does not banish our fear but holds its force with respect and restraint. In the words of the historian of religion Lee Yearley, "Courage, then, consists in having a character that lets neither fear nor over-confidence unduly change behavior."

Courage involves personal determination to act, even in the face of obstacles. Courageous behavior takes many shapes. Personal courage is displayed when we act at the risk of physical injury or bodily harm. Moral courage supports authenticity and integrity—for example, our willingness to express an unpopular view or to stand up to authority by "speaking truth to power." Psychological courage is required as we confront our own destructive habits or struggle to resolve difficult interpersonal conflict. And the researcher Tobias Gritemeyer has identified civic courage as brave behavior that supports social norms and political integrity, even in the face of personal risk.

Alasdair MacIntyre points to the connection of courage with care. When persons we care for or values we cherish are threatened, we rise to their defense. Courage, MacIntyre notes, is the "capacity to risk harm or danger to oneself" in the expression of our care. The most universal example is that of parents who spontaneously—and courageously—will confront any adversary to protect their children. Often it is anger that fuels this dangerous mission of care.

Thomas Aquinas suggested that early in human history the virtue of courage was aligned with the willingness to attack—the aggressive courage of the warrior. Yet over the course of human history courage has more often been expressed in patient endurance, in "not allowing oneself to be made inordinately sorrowful." Aquinas recognized sadness and grief as unavoidable emotions in the face of life's many losses. He acknowledged that sadness can spiral down into melancholy and depression. Patience protects us from this dangerous descent. Patience is the steadying capacity that allows us to stay with our commitments, even in the face of threats and doubts. Josef Pieper concludes, "Patience keeps [persons] from the danger that their spirit may be broken by grief and lose its greatness."

Courage is not simply fearlessness. Initially we become aware of risk, the possibility of injury or other negative consequences. This assessment naturally evokes fear, the emotional arousal that alerts us to danger. Next comes the question of action—what response, by myself or others, might overcome or alleviate the danger. Here fear's arousal supports courage, prompting us to respond through personal action or by recruiting allies.

Our experience of courage is characteristically complex. Psychologists note that this strength of character involves bravery, integrity, and vitality. Bravery names the moral strength to confront difficulty and hardship. Integrity points to our capacity for commitment, even in the face of opposition. Vitality identifies the sense of "being alive" that comes when we are in touch with our deepest values.

Courage as Perseverance

Courage is also registered as perseverance, a virtue celebrated throughout the Bible. The Psalms return often to the theme of perseverance in suffering. "For you, God, have tested us, have tried us as silver is tried. . . . We went through fire and through water. Yet you have brought us out to a spacious place" (Psalm 66:10, 12). The earliest Christians, contending with hostile governments, encouraged one another in this virtue. In his letter to James, Paul returns again and again to the virtue of perseverance. "We also glory in our suffering, because we know that suffering produces perseverance" (James 5:3). And again, "Let perseverance finish its work so that you may be mature and complete, not lacking in anything" (1:4).

Our generation has been privileged to observe a dramatic example of perseverance in the career of Nelson Mandela. Surviving twenty-seven years of imprisonment on Robben Island, Mandela emerged neither subdued nor embittered. Released from prison at age seventy-two, he went on to be elected president of South Africa. From that position he orchestrated the end of social apartheid and initiated the Truth and Reconciliation process that brought social healing to his country. Mandela's resilience is registered dramatically in the vibrant hope that continued to characterize his personal life while in prison, as well as in his subsequent ability to rally his nation to a new vision of political freedom.

The Calming Mood of Contentment

We associate the strength of resilience with perseverance in the face of adversity. Another personal resource—contentment—serves to balance the emotional demands of patient endurance. Contentment names a particular frame of mind—the delight of resting in appreciation of "what is now." In the midst of arduous pursuit of ideals and goals, we do well to take time to savor the goodness already available to us. Even the small successes of our efforts deserve to be celebrated. Taking the time to appreciate these achievements, we welcome the healing emotion of contentment.

This mood—part delight and part relief—often arises at the conclusion of some significant work. In contentment there is no temptation to gloat; we need not calculate margins of victory. Instead, we simply rest in appreciation of what has been brought to life. In Barbara Fredrickson's judgment, contentment prompts people "to savor the moment or recent experiences, feel *oneness* with others or the world around them, and integrate current and recent experiences into their overall self-concept and worldview." Contentment enhances life as it "serves to encourage integration of self with environment, thus expanding our view of the world." Contentment carves out time to focus on the blessings we have received, and supports our readiness to give thanks. In these ways contentment *broadens and builds* our resources.

Feeling content is akin to the emotion of satisfaction. Both emotions encourage us to interrupt our busy schedules, so that we might take pleasure in what has just transpired. *Satisfaction* adds to contentment a judgment of *enough* (*satis* in the Latin language). We experience satisfaction in a job well done or a difficult task completed—even against the odds. This interior instinct alerts us: now it is time to slow down, to acknowledge what has been achieved, to relish this sense of completion, before we turn to the demands of the rest of our life.

Contentment is enhanced in our appreciation of what Michael Leunig calls our *noble tiredness*. "Tiredness is one of our strongest, most noble and instructive feelings. . . . It is an important aspect of our conscience and must be heeded or else we will not survive." He continues, "When you are tired—you must rest like the trees and animals do . . . and enjoyment will surely follow." Learning to honor our vulnerability and personal limitations, we may be surprised by the accompanying stirrings of contentment. Here, too, lifelong resilience is at play.

Resources

Gabrielle Giffords's reflections on resilience appeared in "The Lessons of Physical Therapy," *New York Times*, January 8, 2014.

Nelson Mandela describes his experiences of incarceration and recovery in his autobiography *Long Walk to Freedom*

(New York: Little, Brown, 1994); see also his collection of essays *Conversations with Myself* (New York: Farrar, Straus and Giroux, 2010).

Gina O'Connell Higgins examines the dynamics of recovery and resilience in *Resilient Adults: Overcoming a Cruel Past* (San Francisco: Jossey-Bass, 1994).

George Vaillant's comments are drawn from his essay "Positive Emotions, Spirituality and the Practice of Psychiatry," *Mental Health, Spirituality and the Practice of Psychiatry* 6 (2008): 48–62.

Alex J. Zautra and John W. Reich explore the connections between resilience and the positive emotions in their essay "Resilience: The Meanings, Methods, and Measures of a Fundamental Characteristic of Human Adaptation" in *The Oxford Handbook of Stress, Health, and Coping*, ed. Susan Folkman (New York: Oxford University Press, 2011).

Lee Yearley discusses courage in *Mencius and Aquinas: Theories of Virtue and Conceptions of Courage* (Albany: State University of New York Press, 1990).

Joseph Pieper explores courage as a virtue in *The Four Cardinal Virtues* (South Bend, IN: University of Notre Dame Press, 1966).

See also Tobias Gritemeyer's discussion of the social and political dimensions of courage in his article "Civil Courage," *Journal of Positive Psychology* 2 (2007): 115–19.

On contentment, see Michael Leunig's *Curly Pajama Letters* (Melbourne: Viking Australia, 2006).

Chapter Three

Resilience and the Faces of Power

Personal Power as a Foundation of Resilience

Stir up your power, O Lord, and come.

In this Advent prayer we invoke God's power, opening ourselves to its influence. And along life's journey, our sense of personal power matures in both virtue and confidence. Resilience reflects this growing sense of personal self-efficacy—an awareness of myself as strong, as capable, as active participant in the events that affect me. Resilience both nurtures and reflects personal power. And resilience supports the expectation that hard work and perseverance will lead to a positive outcome.

But for many of us the experience of our own power can be unnerving, especially its expression in anger or violence. Our social imaginations, too, are wounded by the devastating memories of power: the overshadowing cloud of Hiroshima; the scent of Auschwitz; the media's scenes of battles in Vietnam and Afghanistan. Power seems demonic, so often destructive. As these memories gather, Lord Acton's negative judgment of power gains credibility: "Power tends to corrupt, and absolute power corrupts absolutely." Then surely both maturity and holiness must require that we avoid power and its corruptions. But even as we cling to safer ideals of meekness and humility of heart, we sense we have succumbed to too-narrow a view. Can power be rescued from this solely negative interpretation? Power is destructive —and creative; power is demonic—and holy. Our challenge is to acknowledge this rich ambiguity, so that power may be embraced as a resource in Christian life.

In the Hebrew Scripture, Yahweh is addressed by name as Power. The gospel stories of the New Testament display God's power, which becomes tangible in the challenging words and healing actions of Jesus. Reflecting on these scriptural resources, we may recover a nuanced appreciation of power. This exploration will help us acknowledge our own resources, as our real but limited strengths grow into reliable virtues.

Personal power points to an awareness of *myself as strong*, the ways I find myself capable or coercive in interaction with others. Social power refers to the broader experiences of *strength among* us—the energy of this group, the authority of this organization. Social power also involves an awareness of the differences in strength among us—what these differences are and how we will deal with them.

The Faces of Personal Power

We are brought face to face with power as adults. Care, conflict, and control—each is an experience of power through which we influence one another. And the complexity of our lives demands that we become comfortable in expressing our power in a variety of ways.

Power On

As adults we are often challenged to initiate actions ourselves and to influence other people. "Things happen because of me." My action may seem simple: I find I can make another person smile. But the exercise of my influence may be more complex: I propose a new production strategy at the work site, and this suggestion receives serious consideration. Or in a troubled friendship, I take the risk of making a direct confrontation—one that moves our relationship to a deeper level.

Power on is the most direct face of power. I recognize that my actions make a difference. I am more than a child or a passive victim. I can influence my world—at least in some ways. This experience of power does not yet confront the difference between care and constraint nor the tension between influence and coercion.

But even this simplest form of power is not always easy to attain. A variety of factors can defeat this personal strength. A dominating parent may so manage my life that I am left with no sense of personal autonomy. I am cared for, but I cannot shape my own world. Or poverty may educate me in impotence: I am too weak, too ineffectual to influence others. I am encouraged to see myself as a victim, unable to be powerful except, perhaps, in self-destructive acts of violence.

Through the experience of *power on*, I come to sense that I am an agent in my own life and that I have resources that enable me to influence my environment. My strength is not simply "housed" within me; it moves beyond me to influence people and events. I am strong enough to have an impact.

This basic sense of my own autonomy and adequacy leads to an appreciation of my particular competence: I do some things well. Having a skill, mastering a difficult task, being able to bring a project to completion—each of these can bring with it a perception of myself as having resources upon which both I and others can rely. This sense of effectiveness gives me confidence to take on the responsibilities of adult life, both in love and in work. I become more resilient.

Power Over

Resilient people are also able to take charge. Many of the responsibilities of daily life require this kind of power. Serving on the parish council, disciplining our teenage children, supervising a production team, even returning a defective piece of merchandise—each of these is difficult for me if I have no confidence in the possibility and legitimacy of my giving direction to other people.

But *power over* often arouses suspicion, harboring hints of force and manipulation. Perhaps it is the word *over* that frightens us, conjuring up memories of bullies and bosses who used their power to dominate. For many of us, then, there are old wounds to be healed before we can move comfortably into the realm of exercising power ourselves.

To assume leadership in a group, for example, I must be able to generate and focus energies that go beyond my own. Caring for a family, too, requires the coordination and control of diverse and often conflicting energies. In any role of supervision—as foreman, as teacher, as mentor—I must be able to exercise *power over*. Without this exercise of influence, much of group life seems ineffective. Decisions are not carried out, resources are wasted, energy dissipates. Most of us recognize the importance of this exercise of social power, but we remain uneasy with it. Our ambivalence about *power over* is evident in the very different images and feelings that surround the two functions of coordination and control.

The word *coordination* may call up images of a dance troupe. We are impressed and delighted by the coordination of each dancer's movements in the precision of a company's performance. In coordination we see the harmony of disparate powers unified in a graceful effort.

But *control* evokes more sinister images: arms that hold us tightly, rules that restrict our freedom. It may help to recall that the seemingly effortless coordination of the athlete comes only with exceptional control, exercised again and again in disciplined movement. For both dancer and athlete, tedious repetition and control are concealed in the final performance but are sure supports of its success.

Control remains a suspect exercise of power, and with good reason. In our recent social memory, control has often been exercised with constraint and coercion. Leadership positions have sometimes been used to pursue private gain rather than the common good. In these instances, *power over* loses its necessary nuances of shared goals and mutual accountability. Here power becomes a mask for manipulation.

To remind ourselves that the exercise of control is not always manipulative, we might recall the power of the conductor in an orchestra or of the director in a play. Each role requires the ability to focus a group's energies, to channel diverse resources into an organic whole. For the group to be successful, the leader must have control. But the leader's control exists in context. Both the conductor and the musicians are accountable to the musical score. The goal of the joint effort provides the criterion by which the leader's control can be judged. When *power over* is exercised in this way, in pursuit of a common goal and in the context of mutual accountability, we are able to resist the temptation toward manipulation. Resilience—both personal and communal—is often the fruit of this use of power.

Power Against

A third mode of power, equally troublesome for many of us, takes its stance *against*. Here power assumes a combative stance of struggle and opposition, even antagonism. Here I experience my strength when challenged by other people or by the circumstances and obstacles I encounter. At issue is whether I will be found adequate to the test, whether—in the face of outside forces—my own strength will prevail.

This experience of power is part of competitive games, where I match my strength and skill against that of an opponent. Winning, having my power prevail, is important to me here. But as I learn to play well, I come to recognize that winning is not the only benefit involved in the game. There is the exhilaration of the contest itself, the opportunity to try my strength and further develop my skill. There is even the mellow lesson that I can lose without being humiliated and I can fail without being shamed. Often the camaraderie of playing against one another is the chief benefit of the game, offering its own kind of companionship and intimacy.

To be able to contest, then, is part of resilience. This resource of personal power contributes not only in competitive sports but even more in the movements of competition, confrontation, and conflict that are part of the exercise of adult responsibility.

Conflict between spouses, struggles between parents and their teenage children, antagonism among different groups in the parish—these are normal and expected dynamics. These conflicts can escalate toward hostility and hatred: this is part of our fear of power used *against*. But conflict is not inevitably destructive. This powerful dynamic in shared life can be harnessed in ways that turn its energy to good use, redistributing influence among us, revitalizing our commitment to one another, suggesting fresh alternatives for the future.

To deal maturely with these dynamics of competition and conflict I must be somewhat comfortable with the experience of myself as powerful. I must know that I am strong enough to stand in the face of another person's power and survive. I must be comfortable with my own power, trusting that I can handle my rage and moderate my self-interest. This conviction supports my resilience as I enter the social arena with other powerful adults.

Power For

I also come to a sense of personal power in an awareness that "I am strong for others." Many responsibilities of adulthood call on this special kind of strength. As a coworker, I give my talent to the tasks of the team. As a parent, I marshal my resources to care for my children. As a group leader, I use my influence to further our common goals. My ability to have an impact and to make a difference is focused outside myself. I spend myself and my resources in pursuit of someone else's benefit.

At its best, this impulse is expressed in nurturance. I am powerful enough to participate in creating something new—our child or a joint project or a shared dream. Beyond this movement of creativity, I can use my power in care, in support of this new life on its own terms. The crucial difference here, of course, is *on its own terms*. The challenge of nurturance is to be able to use my power for others in ways that empower them, rather than leave them more dependent on me.

We sense how tricky this can be for the parent, to care for growing children not by forcing them to become "my best idea" of who they should turn out to be but fostering their growth into the persons they are in their own right. The task is no less tricky for the business manager or the psychological counselor or the pastoral minister. Our responsibilities require us to use our power for other adults. We come in touch with the ambiguity involved in the use of our power "for their sake." Here we face the tension between care and constraint.

Mature relationships between adults are characterized by mutuality, even where strict equality is neither necessary nor possible. We cannot be exactly equal in intelligence, physical strength, social graces, and other abilities. The challenge of mutuality invites us to become engaged with each other's strengths and weaknesses. Thus *power for* remains an important resource of adult maturity. When the arrogance of "I know better than you what is in your best interests" can be recognized, the strengths of generative care can be released. These sources of personal resilience are essential for the responsibilities of parenting; they are crucial in religious leadership as well.

Power With

Resilient individuals embrace the conviction that "we are strong together." For the benefits of interdependence to be available to me I must first *be able to depend on others*. This capacity for dependence is not the kind of *dependency* so feared by most Americans—the inability to care for my own needs that leaves me at the mercy of others. It is not the dependency that therapists see in the person who characteristically uses his needs to manipulate those around him.

Rather it is the strength of dependence: I am strong enough to be open to and benefit from others' power. Because I know myself to be (somewhat) strong, I can allow my weaknesses to be visible to myself and to others as well. My weaknesses are not stronger than my strengths. So I need not become consumed in the endless and futile effort to hide my limitations: I need not deplete my strength in self-defense.

This sense of *power with* may be experienced in both love and collaboration. We count on each other to bring different resources to our common task. We rely on one another's strengths to make up for the limits we each have. And beyond this, we are aware that when we come together, there is power available that goes beyond what was originally ours. These resources of shared power support our resilience.

Power and Weakness

Any serious discussion of personal resilience must acknowledge both power and weakness. Adult life does not simply lead us out of impotence into strength. Maturity asks, instead, a befriending of ourselves as both weak and strong.

The image of strength in weakness is not unfamiliar to the Christian. The Gospels tell a story of strength and failure: Jesus' power to call us to pursue the Reign of God was not lessened by his inability to protect himself from death. "He was crucified through weakness, and still he lives now through the power of God" (2 Corinthians 13:4).

Paul's letters explore and celebrate, with a special enthusiasm, the paradox of power and weakness in Christian life. At the end of his second letter to the Christians at Corinth, Paul reveals a personal difficulty: this strong, assertive minister was afflicted by "a thorn in the flesh." Troubled and humiliated, he prayed to God to remove this distress from his life. But his weakness did not disappear. In its enduring presence Paul sensed God's response: "My power is at its best in weakness" (12:9). Not "my power will overcome your weakness," nor "my power is unconcerned with weakness," but "my power is *at its best* in weakness." This divine response led Paul to announce to those in Corinth, "I am quite content with my weaknesses . . . for it is when I am weak that I am strong" (12:10).

Even if we are not quite content with our weaknesses, we can at least affirm that God has sometimes worked through them. Often we accomplish things due to our abilities, and we give thanks. And not infrequently our abilities fail us; we are not strong enough to meet some challenge or problem. And yet, despite our failure, the problem or challenge is met. Nor is it that God ignores our limitations. Often enough, God's graceful results seem to emerge directly through our weakness.

Very gradually we embrace the Christian paradox of power. We are intended to grow strong and to become virtuous, and we are called to befriend those enduring weaknesses that God sees fit to leave with us and through which God delights to act. Graceful resilience will follow.

Resources

We discussed links between power and virtue in *Christian Life Patterns* (New York: Crossroad, 1992) and in *Seasons of Strength: New Visions of Adult Christian Maturing* (Lincoln, NE: I-Universe, 2003). We later returned to questions of the complexity of power and authority in *The Emerging Laity* (New York: Doubleday, 1986).

We have learned much from Elizabeth Janeway's *Powers of the Weak* (New York: Knopf, 1981), and Richard Sennett's *Authority* (New York: Vintage Books, 1981).

Chapter Four

Social Resilience— Crisis and Adaptability

Holding Environments— Loyalty and Flexibility

Social resilience is the capacity to foster, engage in, and sustain relationships and to endure and recover from life stressors and social isolation.

—Janet Ramsey and Rosemary Blieszner, *Spiritual Resiliency and Aging*

Resilience is a personal capacity tested and refined in the multiple relationships of our lives. Resilience implies more than autonomy; this resource does not survive and thrive in isolation from other people. The term *social resilience* emphasizes this relational dimension. Relationships are an arena in which the flexible strength of personal resilience is crafted and contested.

The resource of social resilience is rooted in the early nurturing experience that the child psychologist D. W. Winnicott described as a "holding environment." In his research setting Winnicott observed the behavior of a small child playing alone with her toys. Her mother was sitting unobtrusively at a distant corner of the room, within sight but making no direct physical or vocal contact with her child at play. Yet in this unfamiliar research setting, deprived of immediate contact with the parent, the child exhibited no sense of danger or distress. Winnicott identifies this setting as a "holding environment," in which the child learns to feel safe outside the direct presence of the protective parent. This *pretend exercise* of independence strengthens the child for broader engagement in life. The resources of assertion and self-confidence nurtured here are building blocks of resilience.

Our early experiences at school are meant to provide a similar holding environment. Embedded in this supportive setting, guided by attentive teachers, we begin the task of gathering and sharing information and skills. Within this environment we experiment with a new identity as a student, earning grades that measure our wit and resilience. And for many of us religious belonging provides something similar. In the supportive atmosphere of a community of faith, we hear accounts of courageous ancestors ("faith of our fathers") and repeat rituals that embody the collective strength of this religious family. Through these gatherings—educational, religious, civic—we ourselves become more adept at meeting the challenges that life presents, even as we continue to rely on the resilience of others.

For some of us, programs offering support for recovery from abuse and addiction provide a significant holding environment. In these protective enclaves, persons previously wounded are able to take responsibility for their lives, while depending on the support of others. And we all grow stronger as we witness these stories of hard-won journeys of resilience.

For others, time with a psychological counselor or spiritual guide provides the safe setting in which to explore the movement of our life's journey. Graced by the presence of this more experienced person, we often become more confidently aware of our own resources. Their encouragement and guidance support our efforts to live with greater freedom and resilience.

In medieval Christianity, churches often served as sanctuaries in which a distressed person could find refuge. Today many locations—a meeting of Alcoholics Anonymous, a counselor's office, the gathering of a prayer group—may serve as sanctuary—a privileged place where our usual composure is no longer necessary. In such safe havens many of us begin the work of recovering our resilience. As we transition from childhood through the multiple arenas of adolescence and adult life, this scenario is played out again and again. And our resilience in later life will largely depend on the support and affirmation we continue to receive from the communities that surround us with care and compassion.

Two Shipwrecks: Parable of Resilience

In 1864 two storm-wrecked ships were cast up on different coasts of the same inhospitable island, where each would spend the next year unaware of the other. The crew of one ship "abandoned formalities from the past and adopted group problem solving." They worked together to find food and water, constructed shelters and finally built a small boat that brought them to safety. The second crew "retained the formal hierarchy that served them so well on the high seas." On the island they "fought and splintered, lost 16 of the 19 to cold or hunger," and the three survivors were only rescued by chance.

This account illumines a distinctive feature of social resilience. To prevail in the midst of unexpected challenges demands a flexibility that risks disloyalty to traditional ways of performing. As in the example of the successful crew above, a group's survival may at times require "*departing from* the usual ways of thinking."

Institutions and organizations depend, to a large measure, on their members' commitment to established patterns of pursuing common ideals. Thus loyalty serves as a central virtue in social life. Yet in times of crisis new demands challenge established patterns; novel possibilities may lead beyond traditional patterns of behavior. Facing such trying circumstances, where does loyalty stand? In a religious institution such as the Catholic Church, loyalty is often measured in terms of adherence to agreed-upon expressions of shared ideals. In times of stress institutional leaders are often tempted to ensure compliance with escalated notions of loyalty: the movement is from "this is how we do it around here," to "this is the way we have always done it," and finally, "this is God's eternal will for this group." In a season of significant social change, the organization's enforcement of loyalty to previous ways will be challenged by the biblical challenge: "Behold, I am doing a new thing. Now it breaks forth. Do you not perceive it?" (Isaiah 42:19).

Roberto Unger notes the tension in every organization between loyalty to accustomed patterns of activity and the adaptability required to set aside these familiar patterns when they no longer serve. Unger captures this organizational challenge in the tension between repetition and novelty: "Repetition [of time-tested procedures] frees energy and time for what we do not yet know how to repeat." In a time of significant change or crisis, a group will be challenged to move beyond repetition of familiar ways. Unger comments that in a time of upheaval, "the mind must also be able to make moves it never made before, according to rules it can formulate, if at all, only after making them. It must, in other words, be capable of not repeating itself." In the most harrowing part of a period of cultural change, a group experiences the tension between loyalty to its traditional ways and the challenge to pursue its deepest ideals while "not repeating" its well-honed and most familiar responses.

An example reinforces Unger's insight. A congregation of Catholic sisters had met every five years for the past century at their headquarters to plan their future and elect new leaders. Over the past few decades fewer new members have joined this congregation from the United States, even as vocations in their missions in Africa increased. Traditionally, all significant meetings of congregational leaders were held in the United States. Recently, and for the first time, this regularly scheduled international meeting was convened in Uganda. Some American members objected to this radical shift. To them, the airfare required to bring so many leaders to this distant place seemed prohibitively expensive. And in addition, meeting in this location would break with an important tradition. But the majority, aware of the gravity of their situation, voted for this continental shift, and found that their congregation was "capable of not repeating itself." In this daring move, the group displayed its resilience.

Unger then turns to the vocabulary of a group's *framework*. "Our activities fall into two classes. Some activities are moves *within* a framework of organization and belief that we take for granted. At the limit, the framework remains unchallenged and even invisible." Here loyalty is expressed, without ambiguity, in adherence to "the way we have always done things." Unger refers to such behavior as "context-preserving activities."

But there will be times that require institutional leaders to deliberate and make decisions *about* the framework itself. Here we enter into what Unger calls "context-transforming activities." Now loyalty becomes more complex: how to balance loyalty to traditional ways of pursuing our ideals with a creative response to new demands? Unger observes that "only when there is a crisis—that is to say, a problem for which the established structure offers no ready-made solution—do we hit against the limits of our present ideas and methods. Only then does the search for alternate ways of thinking begin." It is at this point that a group's resilience is most tested.

Again, an example amplifies Unger's insight. An organization of Catholic brothers had, throughout its history, established educational institutions to be staffed by their own members. But as membership in the congregation continued to diminish, the leadership saw the need to welcome and train lay teachers in the mission of the religious order. Gradually these lay colleagues, imbued with the sense of mission long cherished by the brothers, moved into leadership positions in these schools. Again, Unger's words come to mind. Responding to this crisis, the religious congregation and its schools are now experiencing a season of resilience.

Finally Unger considers the tension between *method* and *vision*. Method, with its repetitions of familiar and reliable activities, is essential to an institution's good order. But in times of travail a group will have to rely on other resources. Method, in Unger's usage, refer to patterns of an organization's behavior that have been distilled from some previously embraced *vision*. In periods of great cultural change, new visions arise to question deeply ingrained methods. In a time of crisis, "only by the painful triumph of vision over method, the periodic subversion of method for the sake of deepening vision, can we hope to advance insight."

As the Second Vatican Council convened in the early 1960s, this international body of the Catholic Church questioned its repeated "method" of celebrating its religious liturgy in the Latin language. For centuries, the use of this common language was cherished as an expression of the universality of the Church: throughout the world, worshiping communities used the same language in ritual and prayer. Loyalty to this ideal and its practical expression went unchallenged. By the mid-twentieth century, however, religious leaders became increasingly aware of the multiethnic and multilingual nature of this international body. The Catholic Church was no longer a predominantly European institution. At this point the goal of fruitful communication challenged the traditional loyalty to a single common language. With a minority of Catholics dissenting—their loyalty nonnegotiably pledged to the earlier ideal—the church altered its style of liturgical prayer. For most Catholics this change signaled the institution's resilience.

Stories, Symbols, Rituals of Belonging and Prevailing

Support and encouragement of family and friends strengthen personal resilience. In networks of belonging we come to trust our ability to survive the difficulties we face, even to prevail. Belonging and prevailing—the heart of resilience—are celebrated in the vibrant symbols and metaphors of our stories and rituals.

"Human beings make sense of the world by telling stories about it." Karen Armstrong, a historian of religion, reminds us that telling stories "is the most natural and the earliest way in which we organize our experience and our knowledge." Families, cultural institutions, and religious organizations often create heroic accounts to describe their origins. Armstrong recognizes the role of story in the meaning-making of our lives: "From the very beginning we invented stories that enabled us to place our lives in a larger setting that revealed an underlying pattern, and gave us a sense that, against all the depressing and chaotic evidence to the contrary, life had meaning and value."

When we tell stories—about our personal life or our family or the larger community—we gather diverse memories into a single narrative thread that displays direction and purpose. From disparate happenings, we create a plot. Prior to this creative assembling, a life may seem little more than a series of disconnected happenings. When these events are gathered into a plot, we recognize their meaning and value. We compose a story line that makes sense of the multiple events of our days.

Stories—personal and cultural, lived and recounted—support enduring and resilient identities. These stories, with their supportive symbols and rituals, *re-mind* us of our best hopes and highest ideals. In memories of hardship and endurance, of courage and creativity, we recall where we belong. In these stories—part history, part myth—a group reinforces its place within a cherished tradition. And members are fortified by these reminders of their group's resilience.

For Christians the biblical text is a repository celebrating a history of resilience. Some chapters recall the endurance of believing communities through persecution and suffering. Other texts recount a group's response to novel challenges, finding resources to adapt to new circumstances. A paradigmatic story of crisis and change appears in the New Testament letter to the Galatians. In a critical moment in the first generation of believers, Peter's conviction that they must remain loyal to the Jewish tradition to which they belonged confronted Paul's intuition that the church should display more flexibility toward those joining the community who were not Jewish. Were kosher dietary rules to be followed by these newcomers? And what of circumcision? This cherished practice, long a requirement for inclusion among God's chosen people, prompted great loyalty among early Jewish converts. But perhaps non-Jews might be exempted from this requirement. Arguments ensued, with powerful leaders at a standoff. Finally agreement was reached—circumcision was not to be required. From that crisis onward the Christian community expanded its sense of identity, welcoming converts of many national identities and ethnic heritages into the Christian faith.

Today in the Catholic Church the drama of social resilience is being played out again. In October 2014, a synod of bishops gathered in Rome to consider the special challenges faced by married couples and families in the contemporary world. As the synod began, Pope Francis invoked the advice of an earlier pope in a similar time of cultural transition. In 1965 Pope Paul VI had written, "By carefully surveying the signs of the times, we are making every effort to adapt ways and methods to the growing needs of our time and the changing conditions of society." The appeal to "the signs of the times" brings to mind the tension of vision and method. As cultures move through history, new visions may question traditional methods and ways of proceeding. Preparations undertaken in advance of the 2014 synod signaled a more inclusive vision of those to be consulted regarding questions of marriage and family. A worldwide census sought information from Catholics everywhere.

When ecclesial decisions are informed in this way—by information gathered broadly from the community of faith—the traditional framework of reflection and decision making begins to change. Earlier understandings of loyalty come under pressure: Must church leaders simply repeat the insights and injunctions of its rich past? Or might they dare, after scrutiny of the signs of the times, to "make moves never made before"?

For all Christians, the range of biblical stories of resilience should offer great consolation. Whatever the crisis, we have been here before—sometimes simply enduring through difficulties, sometimes making significant shifts so as to remain faithful to a deeper vision. The faith community has survived over two thousand years, a testimony to its resilience. In times of cultural change, reminding ourselves that adversity has played a central role in the Christian story supports our openness to the action of the Spirit now.

Resources

The quotation from Janet Ramsey and Rosemary Blieszner is from *Spiritual Resiliency and Aging: Hope, Relationality, and the Creative Self* (Amityville, NY: Baywood, 2012).

D. W. Winnicott discusses "the holding environment" in *Home Is Where We Start From* (New York: Norton, 1986).

The account of the two ships appears in John Cacioppo, Harry Reis, and Alex Zautra, "Social Resilience: The Value of Social Fitness with an Application to the Military," *American Psychologist* 66 (January 2011): 43–51; see 44.

Roberto Unger explores the dynamics of social resilience in *The Self Awakened* (Cambridge, MA: Harvard University Press, 2007).

Karen Armstrong, *A Short History of Myth* (New York: Canongate, 2005). Also see her *The Great Transformation: The Beginning of Our Religious Traditions* (New York: Knopf, 2006).

On the 2014 Catholic synod on marriage and the family, see Elisabetta Povoledo, "Pope Francis Beatifies an Earlier Reformer, Paul VI," *New York Times*, Monday, October 20, 2014.

Chapter Five

Spiritual Resilience—
The Transformation of Adversity
Resources of Belonging and Resistance

*You who have made me see many troubles and
calamities will revive me again. From the
depths of the earth you will bring me up again.*

—Psalm 71:20

I am Malala. On a Tuesday morning in October 2012 Malala Yousafzai boarded a bus to go to school in the Swat district of Pakistan. A gunman followed the young Pashtun girl onto the bus and fired at her three times. One bullet hit the left side of Malala's forehead, traveled the length of her face and entered her shoulder. Despite the severity of her wounds, the fifteen-year-old rallied under the care of physicians, first in Pakistan and then at Queen Elizabeth Hospital in Birmingham, England. This tragedy provoked widespread support both for Malala and for her commitment to education for all children.

Malala's resilience was remarkable. Once recovered from her wounds, she began to speak out, taking advantage of the international platform that the assassination attempt had provided for her. But public speaking was not something new for this teenager. From an early age Malala had been encouraged by her father to speak up. When she was only ten years of age, he had taken her to Peshawar to address the local press club. Three years before the attack she had written a blog for the BBC, detailing her life under Taliban rule and her hope that education would be more widely available to girls in Pakistan.

Malala's resilience was rooted in a distinctive sense of belonging and prevailing. At birth her father had named her after Malalai, the woman acknowledged as "the greatest heroine of Afghanistan." This nineteenth-century woman warrior had given her life in rallying Afghan troops in their victory over the British. This brave woman died in battle, but her cause—the liberation of her people—nevertheless prevailed. Malala's father never tired of retelling the story of Malalai, reminding his daughter of the tradition of valiant women to which she belonged. This historical model nurtured Malala's resilience.

Renewed Interest in Spiritual Resilience

Spirituality has long been a suspect category in the realms of scholarship. Associated with displays of emotional enthusiasm, spirituality seemed at best a poor cousin of theology. Relegated to the realm of personal piety, spirituality seemed of little practical value to the modern world.

Psychologists today are interested in the role of spirituality in adult development and maturity. Robert Emmons is a leader in the fields of personality psychology and the psychology of religion. From an earlier research focus on the personal goals that contribute to a person's well-being or happiness, he has turned to a more systematic study of the role of spirituality in psychological health and flourishing. He writes, "It is my belief that the psychological sciences are on the verge of a spiritual revolution. . . . Research that documents the role of spirituality in personal and social well-being will play a major role in this revolution."

Emmons offers this definition: "Spirituality . . . is thought to encompass a search for meaning, for unity, for connectedness, for transcendence." He added: "Embedding one's finite life within a grander, all-encompassing narrative appears to be a universal human need, as the inability to do so leads to despair and self-destructive behavior." Emmons sees a "robust connection between personal well-being and a concern for the spiritual." The *faith factor* emerges as a significant contributor to quality-of-life indicators such as life satisfaction, happiness, self-esteem, hope, and optimism, and meaning in life. George Vaillant elaborates on this sense of belonging: "I argue that spirituality reflects humanity's biological press for connection and community building as much as it reflects the individual's need for sacred revelation."

Spiritual resilience is a capacity waiting to be developed: a discipline of honing hope and trusting the world. John Cottingham writes, "To love morally, courageously, generously, while facing the unavoidable fragility of our human lives, we need a continuing programme of spiritual askesis [asceticism], which will replace fear with trust, which will address our vulnerability by transforming it into a receptivity, an openness, a willingness to become like the child that is intimately present deep within the adult life of each of us."

Spiritual resources support resilience in the lives of many people. Here spirituality encompasses more than adherence to the beliefs and practices of a particular religion. In their research on sources of resilience, for example, Janet Ramsey and Rosemary Blieszner identify spirituality as "an affective, cognitive, and experiential relationship with the powerful, gracious, life-giving Source of all being."

The psychologist Kenneth Pargament has written extensively about the contribution of religious beliefs and practices to resilience, and his findings are supported by the work of many other scholars. Religious beliefs provide sources of meaning that help us look beyond the negative circumstances that sometimes engulf us. Religious symbols offer images of a deeper order in human life, in which evil and suffering are recognized as real but not ultimate.

Images of a just and benevolent God encourage believers to seek religious support in the midst of personal distress. Praying to God, reflecting on the exemplary lives of holy persons, meditating on sacred texts, participating in religious rituals—these activities are consistently associated with positive psychological outcomes. But evidence also shows that spiritual struggles can sometimes make matters worse. When tragedy strikes, believers may become enraged that the all-powerful Deity has permitted such destruction. Or they may fear that, due to their own sins, the just God has abandoned them. Yet in contemporary research these maladaptive interpretations of suffering appear much less frequently than the religious responses that emphasize hope and gratitude.

Spiritual Resilience and Belonging

In the preceding chapter we explored the role of resilience in developing bonds that support group allegiance. Spiritual resilience supports a yet deeper search for meaning. Humans yearn for assurance that the world we inhabit makes sense, that it holds together and holds out meaning and purpose. We hope that our lives might be part of some large quest for significance.

The anthropologist Clifford Geertz acknowledges that this hope is tested by events that "raise the uncomfortable suspicion that perhaps the world, and hence man's life in the world, has no genuine order at all . . . no moral coherence." Religious traditions and spiritual paths address this challenge by "the formulation, by means of symbols, of an image of such a genuine order of the world which will account for, and even celebrate, the perceived ambiguities, puzzles, and paradoxes of human experience." For Geertz "the effort is not to deny the undeniable—that there are unexplained events, that life hurts, or that rain falls on the just—but to deny that there are inexplicable events, that life is unendurable, and that justice is a mirage."

For many of us as Christians, the biblical stories of life and death, of loss and gain, of suffering and redemption, weave a pattern of meaning and purpose that provides a foundation for resilience. As these stories resonate with our life experience, we gain confidence in the assurance of our capacity for resilience.

Biblical Stories of Spiritual Resilience

The history of the Jews, our religious ancestors, is a story of continuous and dramatic resilience. And it is a story that illumines the inner dynamics of believing and prevailing that are at the core of this human capacity.

The Jews believed in a story—an account, part history and part myth, of their being chosen by their God to live and survive. "Chosen" did not mean better than, but rather special enough—worthy of surviving, despite all their flaws and infidelities before Yahweh. Belief lay at the center of their resilience in the face of the ghettos and pogroms that mark their long history. With nothing to believe in, a people does not survive. Belief leads, in turn, to prevailing. Here again how one survives is important. For the Jewish people, prevailing did not mean military victory over the ancient Romans, or medieval Europeans, or German Nazis. Prevailing meant survival through every hellish disaster, and the promise of an ultimate flourishing.

The resilience of the Jewish people lies in the indulgence of their God. Whatever their folly or sinfulness, God extended forgiveness and rescued his people from the wretchedness they endured. And their resilience grew out of their suffering: "You, O God, have tested us; you have tried us as silver is tried . . . we went through fire and water, yet you have brought us out to a spacious place" (Psalm 66). And "you who have made me see many troubles and calamities will revive me again, from the depths of the earth you will bring me up again" (Psalm 71).

In the biblical account of Jacob wrestling in the dark with an unknown assailant we meet an extraordinary example of resilience. In the middle of the night Jacob is attacked by someone or something that throws him to the ground. As they struggle, his opponent "touched the hollow of his thigh and Jacob's thigh was put out of joint as he wrestled with him." But Jacob had a firm hold on his assailant who then pleaded, "Let me go for the day is breaking." And Jacob replied that he would let his opponent go if he would bless him. So the assailant blessed Jacob and gave him a new name. "Your name will no more be Jacob, but Israel, for you have struggled with God and with humans, and you have prevailed" (Genesis 32:30). As the sun came up, it dawned on Jacob that he had been wrestling with his God. He limps away from this mysterious encounter, bearing both an injured thigh and a new identity. And in this embrace of his injury, Jacob prevailed.

The Role of Faith in Spiritual Resilience

Faith is a human capacity, a way of seeing the world that is registered both in the trust we place in reliable companions and in the conviction that life itself makes sense. In the spiritual exercise of faith we put our trust in a cause larger than our individual lives. This faith supports a sense of belonging among believers and a commitment to prevailing in the long-term projects that we pursue as worthy of our best effort, even in the face of setbacks and disappointments.

Faith is often associated with religious belonging. For much of human history many have found a religious tradition—Christianity, Judaism, Buddhism, Islam—as the setting in which they were schooled in the ways of faith. These supportive communities offered stories and symbols of meaning and purpose. These gatherings of believers served as "holding environments" within which a person's faith might mature and ripen. Through the beliefs of this particular religious group, a person would develop faith in life itself and commitment to the virtues of compassion and justice. Religion has been the customary residence of faith, just as marriage has functioned as the customary home of committed love. But just as love is experienced beyond romance and family, faith can be expressed beyond religious belonging.

The faith that lies at the core of spiritual resilience is rooted in the human imagination. This conviction does not suggest that faith is a mere illusion or simply an invention of the pious. Instead, we are reminded that it is by imagination that we perceive—even create—worlds of meaning to which we commit our resilient selves. With the aid of our imagination we come to recognize purposes and larger meanings that others might not appreciate; and we recognize in others a companionship that might not be obvious to all.

Gina O'Connell Higgins describes faith as "a uniquely human capacity to locate and create images and symbols in the service of sustaining our faith in a larger future." Looking back at their fraught history, the Jewish people came to see their ancestors' sojourn in the desert as a metaphor for all the episodes of dryness and disorientation that we humans undergo. Through the power of imagination Jews have come to recognize this exile as a master image of the many ways that humanity becomes separated from the nourishment and comfort of a homeland, geographic or spiritual. Early Christians continued this exploration of the religious imagination, especially through the parables of the gospel. We are reminded that seeds fall into the ground and die, but from this perishing comes new life. This insight alerts the faith community to the rhythm of dying-and-rising that is proclaimed in the Paschal Mystery.

Resilience depends on the ability to interpret our life journey anew, to see beyond the injuries that would defeat us, past the failures of our religious and cultural traditions that so repeatedly fail us. By reframing this history, we renew our faith in life; by seeing through temporary setbacks, we reclaim our resilience. Without the imaginative capacity of faith, we are left with a world devoid of transformations, a world confined by "what you see is what you get." Such a climate leads to the death of the spirit.

Returning to the story of Malala, we recognize spiritual resilience in an expanded vision of belonging and prevailing. This young girl learned that she belonged to a fiercely proud people. This realization provided courage to spend herself in promoting education for girls, even in the face of fierce religion-based opposition. She had learned that her name-sake hero a century before had not simply *lost her life* in a struggle for freedom, but had *given her life* in a cause that was more significant than her individual survival. American citizens, along with many others throughout the world, recognize this same scenario in the life of Martin Luther King Jr. Acknowledging the tragedy of his assassination, we do not simply say he *lost his life*. Rather he *gave his life* to the cause of racial justice that outlives him.

Resources

Malala Yousafzai, with Christina Lamb, *I Am Malala* (New York: Little, Brown, 2013).

See, for example, Bruce W. Smith, J. Alexis Ortiz, Kathryn T. Wiggins, Jennifer F. Bernard, and Jeanne Dalen "Spirituality,

Resilience, and Positive Emotions," in *The Oxford Handbook of Psychology and Spirituality*, ed. Lisa J. Miller (New York: Oxford University Press, 2012).

Also see Steven Southwick and Dennis Charney, *Resilience: The Science of Mastering Life's Greatest Challenges* (New York: Cambridge University Press, 2012).

Janet Ramsey and Rosemary Blieszner, *Spiritual Resiliency and Aging: Hope, Relationality and the Creative Self* (Amityville, NY: Baywood, 2012).

Robert Emmons, *The Psychology of Ultimate Concern* (New York: Guilford Press, 1999).

See George Vaillant's *Spiritual Evolution: A Scientific Defense of Faith* (New York: Doubleday, 2009) and "Positive Emotions, Spirituality and the Practice of Psychiatry," *Mental Health, Spirituality and the Practice of Psychiatry* 6 (2008): 48–62.

The historian Simon Schama tells this story of resilience in his two-volume study *The Story of the Jews* (New York: HarperCollins, 2013).

Clifford Geertz explores the links between the search for meaning and spiritual resilience in *Available Light: Anthropological Reflections on Philosophical Topics* (Princeton, NJ: Princeton University Press, 2008), esp. 192.

Gina O'Connell Higgins, *Resilient Adults: Overcoming a Cruel Past* (San Francisco: Jossey-Bass, 1994), esp. 171 for the quotation.

Chapter Six

A Soldier's Resilience— Strength and Vulnerability

Healing Wounds, Building Resilience

Younger soldiers won't truly believe that they can seek help without destroying their careers until top generals and senior sergeants begin to publicly share stories of their own struggles with combat stress, PTSD, and depression.

—Yochi Dreazen, *The Invisible Front*

If resilience is measured in adversity overcome, this strength should stand as an essential resource of those in military service. Adversity is the occupational arena of the soldier, both in basic training and in combat. Military resilience is displayed in the individual soldier's ability to face down lethal threats on a daily basis, and in the troop's continued performance under pressure, succumbing neither to panic nor retreat.

The wars in Iraq and Afghanistan have brought to light two crucial tensions in the development of military resilience. A soldier is trained to be confident and strong; yet when severely disabled by PTSD, he or she is expected to expose his or her suffering—vulnerability—to authorities who decide whether the soldier is fit to continue in the service. "The primary message they received in basic training, ROTC, and military academies such as West Point was that mental illness was a sign of weakness, and that weak soldiers had no place in the army" (Dreazen, 185).

The soldier has also imbibed the ethic of responsibility for his or her comrades. When one is killed, he or she is likely to feel not only grief but guilt for not providing protection. These conflicts—personal and institutional—raise new questions about resilience in the military.

Stories and Symbols of Military Resilience

Like other institutions, the military turns to stories, symbols, and rituals to develop resilience in its members. At military academies, future leaders are schooled over several years in an ethic of cohesion and flexibility. But in the basic training of enlisted recruits the challenge is steeper. New soldiers must be inducted quickly into the values that define this organizational culture. Putting on the military uniform, the recruit assumes a new identity, becoming a member of a distinctive family. The new soldier is introduced to the organizational hierarchy, with multiple ranks and insignia that define belonging and status. The symbolic language of *semper fi* and *army of one* reinforce the growing conviction that the soldier is strong and resilient, both personally and as part of the military unit.

In his short story collection *Redeployment*, Iraq veteran Phil Klay describes the stories and symbols that instill this sense of belonging. "In boot camp, [instructors] teach you Medal of Honor stories"—stories of heroism, self-sacrifice, patriotism. These stories instruct the new recruits in the glory and costs of inclusion in this esteemed group. Compelling symbols—battalion insignia and awards for valor—reinforce honor, respect, and courage. Motivating slogans are an essential element in this symbolic language: "be all you can be" and "a few good men"—all meant to reinforce pride of belonging and support resilience in combat.

Klay describes a ritual that is meant to reinforce belonging and redefine prevailing. As the body of a deceased companion is carried from the field, soldiers come to attention and salute. At every stage of the body's journey home, military personnel stand silently in the presence of their deceased comrade's coffin. In Klay's moving description: "Everywhere [the body] went, Marines and sailors and soldiers and airmen would have stood at attention as it traveled to the family of the fallen, where the silence, the stillness would end." These symbolic actions both honor the fallen soldier and signify that the army prevails even in the face of individual deaths.

Resilience Tested

Klay captures the emotional mayhem of warfare that puts resilience to the test. The soldiers in his short stories display the mood swings and emotional extremes that are part of military deployment. On hyperalert during patrol, the off-duty soldier typically collapses in boredom—with little opportunity to process the residual emotions of rage, grief, and guilt. A soldier describes the hypervigilance provoked in response to an *orange state of alert*: "Here is what orange is. You don't see or hear like you used to. Your brain chemistry changes. You take in every piece of the environment, everything. I could spot a dime in the street twenty yards away. I had antennae out that stretched down the block."

Exposed to such dangerous settings over time, many soldiers experience an inability to sleep. Some adopt a daily regime of exercise to exhaust their body and tamp down their swirling emotions. Others turn to drugs to help them rest, followed by caffeinated drinks to keep them alert during patrols. This cycle reinforces the mood swings that quickly become chronic. "You exhaust yourself to the point where only pain and euphoria remain." Dexter Filkins salutes Klay's effectiveness in describing "the ways the conflict splintered the psyches of the men who fought and how it rattled around in their minds." The human psyche is not built for this emotional cycle.

The Undoing of Resilience

The exorbitant price of war was traditionally disguised beneath heroic and nationalist rhetoric. At the beginning of the twentieth century patriots could still extol the ancient saying, *sweet and right it is to die for one's country (dulce et decorum est pro patria mori)*. A century of warfare, plus the experience in Iraq and Afghanistan, have put the lie to such rhetoric. George Packer comments, "Both [wars] began with hubris and false victories, turned into prolonged stalemates, and finally deserved the bitter name of defeat." For many soldiers, a conviction that the wars in Iraq and Afghanistan served a higher purpose began to disintegrate;

in its place arose experiences of fragmentation fueled by violent emotions that were difficult to control. This widespread experience of fragmentation was soon diagnosed as posttraumatic stress disorder (PTSD), a shattering of the psyche that often leads to suicide for some who suffer its devastating symptoms.

The resilience of the warrior—tough enough to face down any adversary—does not equip veterans for the return home. In direct military service they have learned that vulnerability and valor are incompatible. To be vulnerable in battle is to let others down, to fail the mission. To be vulnerable to emotions of fear and grief will only weaken one's alertness and willingness to fight. Thus vulnerability can be fatal. As one soldier stated, "There can't be any chinks in the armor." Yet returning home, the soldier is often encouraged to acknowledge personal distress, to seek help from a health professional or chaplain. For many returning members of the military, acknowledging vulnerability—even to oneself— is very difficult. And many fear that any discussion of lingering personal pain or emotional distress will contradict their heroic reputation, perhaps even jeopardize a future career.

Returning veterans, in their poems and short stories, struggled to name this malaise, with its overlay of "brotherhood, alienation from a former self, the ghosts of the past, the misfit of home" (George Packer). Here the image of "home" is no longer a place of welcome and comfort. Veteran Kevin Powers writes in his *Letter Composed during a Lull in the Fighting*, "I am home and whole, so to speak / . . . But I can't remember / how to be alive." Brian Turner repeats this theme: "Home isn't a big enough space for all that I must bring to it. America, vast and laid out from one ocean to another, is not a large enough space to contain the war each soldier brings home. And, even if it could—it doesn't want to."

Conversations between returning veterans and civilians often founder in remarks like "I can't imagine what you have gone through." Although spoken in respect, this response most often shuts down any genuine exchange. In these conversations, Klay notes, "The civilian wants to respect what the veteran has gone through. The veteran wants to protect memories that are painful and sacred to him from outside judgment. But the result is the same: the veteran in a corner by himself, able to proclaim about war but not discuss it, and the civilian shut out from a conversation about one of the most morally fraught activities our nation engages in—war."

"The notion that the veteran is an unassailable authority on the experience of war shuts down conversation." Klay adds, "If we fetishize trauma as incommunicable then survivors are trapped—unable to feel truly known by their non-military friends and family." Klay recounts the obstacles that defeat communication. He describes "the veteran mystique" of one who has seen war. This distances him from those at home: "You weren't there." Arriving back in the United States, the returning veteran feels he or she is both better than these others (having paid the price of defending his or her country) and worse (he or she was involved in horrible events). All this distances him or her from civilians.

A Soldier's Dilemma: Vulnerability

In his accounts of military experience Klay vividly describes the overwhelming sense of vulnerability. In unresolved memories, many military personnel continue to be present to actions and events that haunt them. They feel distant—even alienated—from those who did not serve. Managing this unnamed vulnerability seems to demand building a wall, to isolate themselves as the body of a deceased companion is carried from the field. At times even more self-defeating measures seem necessary: personal vulnerability is defended by the numbing effects of alcohol and by driving others away through uncontrollable flashes of anger.

The tensions generated by unrealistic images of military resilience become obvious in the tragedy of veterans' suicide. Both military leaders and the general public are aware today of the evidence of the escalating number of suicides among returned soldiers. "The military's suicide rate jumped more than 80 percent between 2002 and 2009. In 2012 more soldiers died by their own hand than in combat. In 2013 the total number of military suicides since the start of the wars in Iraq and Afghanistan passed the 1,000 mark" (Dreazen). A scene at the National Mall in Washington in March 2014 illustrates this concern. Volunteers spread out across the mall area, planting small flags to commemorate the 1,892 members of the military who had succumbed to death by suicide since January of that year.

A soldier's suicide has always been seen as an especially horrible death. To die in combat is seen as honorable, but to die by one's own hand was considered the worst kind of surrender, a defeat and a final judgment of a soldier's lack of resilience. Military suicide not only signaled the individual soldier's moral weakness, but symbolically undermined the resilience of the entire troop.

To many military commanders, the debilitating symptoms of PTSD signaled a weakness not too distant from a surrender to suicide—a collapse of the soldier's resilience. This too was a sign of weakness and a source of shame. Both suicide and PTSD often created a stigma for the soldier and his or her family. This has gradually begun to change as more military leaders come forward to acknowledge their own combat-induced mental suffering. In *The Invisible Front*, Yochi Dreazen tells the story of General Mark Graham, his wife Carol, and the deaths of their two sons. Both sons aspired to follow their father into the military. The elder, Jeff, did so and served in Iraq where he was killed by an IED. Months before, his younger brother, Kevin, worried that his antidepression medicine would prevent his enlistment, stopped taking his medicine. A short time later, after a surge of depression, Kevin hanged himself.

His parents were devastated by the death of both sons within a few months. But they were further troubled when Jeff was celebrated as a hero even as, out of embarrassment, friends skirted mentioning Kevin's life (and death). Kevin's suicide began to appear as an early sign of a more ominous trend. During General Graham's first year as commander at Fort Carson in 2008, eight soldiers on the base committed suicide. Graham soon initiated a campaign to challenge the stigma associated with PTSD and suicide. Such an effort, of course, goes against a deeply traditional vision of military resilience.

Dreazen's account concludes on a sober note: "The most important changes, though, are the ones that will be the hardest to put in place because they require fundamental changes to the military's culture and value system." During more than a year of research for his book, Dreazen "was able to identify only three generals who have gone public about their nightmares, jumpiness, flashes of anger, or other PTSD-related symptoms." Sadly, he reported, "even now, at the very pinnacle of their professional lives, most of the generals afflicted with PTSD suffer in silence because they are afraid other soldiers will see them as weak."

Spiritual Resilience and the Military

Military resilience is rooted in troop cohesion and loyalty. Such resilience builds on recruits' personal resources. The goal of military training is to instill "the acceptance of diversity, mutuality, sharing of resources, commitment, and generativity" that will support military morale and effectiveness. And research findings "emphasize the role of connections with other individuals, groups and large collectives as a means of fostering adaptation through new learning and growth." A crucial element here is the soldier's capacity for empathy. Attentive and accurate awareness of what others are feeling is a core skill of individual resilience, and a key ingredient of social resilience.

Perhaps surprisingly, recent research has explored the role in military life of spiritual resilience. Military leaders now recognize the vital links between soldiers' well-being and their embrace of a sustaining vision of life's meaning. Studies sponsored by the US military use the vocabulary of *spiritual fitness* and *religious worldview*. The Air Force defines spiritual fitness as "the ability to adhere to beliefs, principles, or values needed to persevere and prevail in accomplishing tasks." Such fitness does not require an explicit religious identification or articulated belief in the supernatural. In its definition of "spiritual worldview," the Air Force study includes belief in transcendent meaning and purpose, embrace of personal values from which individuals derive peace and comfort, and a sense of meaning or purpose in life. What is supported is a commitment to a set of values for which a person would be willing to risk his or her life. The spiritual or transcendent elements in military life are registered in the language of ultimate sacrifice: the death of the individual soldier must be reframed until it contributes to the prevailing of the army and nation. The rhetoric at military cemeteries contribute to this reframing as they are described as "hallowed ground" and as "consecrated" by the sacrifice of many individuals.

Resilience Reclaimed:
Healing "The Ruins of Character"

In the aftermath of the Vietnam War, psychiatrist Jonathan Shay chronicled ways in which the traumatic memories of military personnel, when denied the opportunity to be acknowledged and exorcised, flared up in nightmares and destructive behaviors. Returning to the Unites States, many soldiers continued behaviors that had been essential to their survival on the battlefield. Some remained in combat mode, unable to shed the hypervigilance and extreme aggressiveness that had once been essential to their survival. At home this "combative behavior" often appeared in sudden rage, inability to sleep, domestic violence, and increasing dependence on alcohol and drugs for relief.

More recently Shay has written explicitly of the moral injury that many military personnel exhibit upon returning from war. This injury may have arisen in following a command that the soldier knew was wrong or in recognizing himself as responsible for the death of an innocent civilian. The distress might be rooted in the larger campaign of violence that is inescapable in wartime. Shay defines moral injury as "a betrayal of what is morally correct." Guilt and shame fuel this sense of an injury that lingers long after one has returned from combat.

Psychotherapists have designed carefully focused group discussions that allowed soldiers to begin the delicate process of transforming unconscious trauma into consciously grieved tragedy. Shay himself gathered small groups of veterans to retell their stories of war in the company of other veterans. In *Achilles in Vietnam* he describes the healing that can occur in such settings: "When a survivor creates a fully realized narrative that brings together the shattered knowledge of what happened, the emotions that were aroused by the meanings of the events, and the bodily sensations that the physical events created, the survivor pieces back together the fragmentation of consciousness that trauma has caused."

When these involuntary recollections were finally shared in a safe therapeutic setting, the toxic memories began to lose their power. Recounting these stories of horror and grief, now honored by being made public, gradually transforms the trauma of their military experiences into tragedy. These still-terrible events are now honored and made more tolerable. A medic returning from Iraq states: "What arose at the retreat for the first time was a deep sense of compassion for my past and present self: compassion for the idealistic, young would-be physician forced to witness unspeakable obscenities of which mankind is capable, and for the haunted veteran who could not let go of memories he could not acknowledge he carried" (Jack Kornfield, "Stopping the War").

Shay describes this transformation: "Recollection brings hidden memories into consciousness; no longer incapacitated by them, we can afford the luxury of remembering." Such therapeutic storytelling, Shay argues, "enables the survivor to rebuild the ruins of character." Through this process, horrendous scars were transformed into honorable wounds. And resilience is reclaimed.

Resources

Phil Klay has created short stories of war in his National Book Award–winning *Redeployment*. Also see his op-ed piece in the *New York Times*, "After War, a Failure of the Imagination," Sunday, February 9, 2014.

David Finkel, in *Thank You for Your Service* (New York: Farrar, Straus and Giroux, 2013) and Yochi Dreazen, in *The Invisible Front* (New York: Crown, 2014) detail the stresses of warfare and how they unravel a soldier's resilience.

Dexter Filkins reviews Klay's book in the essay "The Long Road Home," *New York Times*, Sunday, March 9, 2014.

George Packer discusses the poetry and essays of veterans in "Home Fires," *New Yorker*, April 7, 2014.

On the flag-planting ceremony, see Jada Smith, "Using Flags to Focus on Veteran Suicides," *New York Times*, Friday, March 28, 2014.

Thom Shanker and Richard Oppel's essay "War's Elite Tough Guys, Hesitant to Seek Healing," appeared in the *New York Times*, Friday, June 6, 2014.

See Kevin Powers, *Letters Composed during a Lull in the Fighting: Poems* (New York: Little Brown, 2014), and Brian Turner, *My Life in a Foreign Country: A Memoir* (London: Jonathan Cape, 2014).

Jonathan Shay examines PTSD in *Achilles in Vietnam* (New York: Atheneum, 1994); see especially page 188. Also see *Odysseus in America: Combat Trauma and the Tales of Homecoming* (New York: Scribner, 2003).

On Shay's notion of "moral injury" see Jeff Severns Guntzel, "Beyond PTSD to 'Moral Injury,'" on Krista Tippetts's website, www.onbeing.org.

The quotation from the young medic is found in "Stopping the War," an excerpt from *A Path with Heart,* by Jack Kornfield, at www.yin4men.com.

John Cacioppo, Harry Reis, and Alex Zautra, "Social Resilience: The Value of Social Fitness with an Application to the Military," *American Psychologist* 66 (January 2011): 43–51.

Douglas Yeung and Margret T. Martin have led research reported in the essay "Spiritual Fitness and Resilience: A Review of Relevant Constructs, Measures and Links to Well-Being." This is part of the RAND Project: AIR FORCE Series on Resiliency, 2014.

Chapter Seven

Civic Resilience—
Cultivating Political Emotions

Civic Compassion—Boston and New Orleans

*All societies need to think about compassion
for loss, anger at injustice, the limiting of envy
and disgust in favor of inclusive sympathy.*

—Martha Nussbaum, *Political Emotions*

Boston Strong! April 15, 2013. As runners approached the
finish line of the Boston Marathon, two explosions suddenly
shattered lives and shocked a city's proud tradition. Like the
destruction of the Twin Towers in New York City twelve
years earlier, the message from terrorists was also symbolic:
your civic lives are not safe.

Immediately after the explosions, many in the Boston
crowd surged not away from the bomb cite in self-protection, but
toward the chaotic scene—in compassion. Applying makeshift

tourniquets to stanch bleeding limbs, they rushed the victims to ambulances and hospitals. These courageous actions saved many lives. Almost immediately the city of Boston began a campaign of recovery, signaling its resilience. Soon the rallying cry "Boston Strong!" rose in defiance of the violence.

Precisely one year later, people throughout Boston stood in silence for a moment of commemoration. In memorials to those who died and the salute of those who suffered severe injuries that day, the city transformed a senseless act of violence—a trauma—into a shared tragedy. The terrifying experiences surrounding the event were not forgotten or denied, but honored in the determination to move forward. The civic mantra—*Boston Strong!*—emblazoned on billboards and T-shirts, announced the city's resolve that this violence would not prevail. The recovery of the survivors was nurtured in large part by the support and compassion—the civic resilience—of this city and the nation.

Political Emotions

We often associate emotions with personal lives and link politics exclusively with the public realm. Yet we know that emotions, however unacknowledged or manipulative, are a driving force in political life. The philosopher Martha Nussbaum has been a leading architect in refashioning a more generous vision of the force of human feelings. Her work is representative of a renewed interest in a number of disciplines (philosophy, psychology, ethics, and the neurosciences) in exploring emotion's role in our moral and spiritual lives. In *Political Emotions*, she explores ways in which "love matters for justice."

Nussbaum defines the focus of her discussion: "The nations we are imagining aspire to justice. They want to figure out how emotions can help them in their work, motivating good policies and rendering them stable. They also want to thwart, or at least control, emotions that would derail their efforts."

The historical background of Nussbaum's agenda is important. For centuries European society depended on an indigenous Christian faith, with its arsenal of virtues—especially altruistic love and compassion—to motivate citizens to patriotic self-sacrifice for the good of the nation. This union of religion and politics (identified in European history as *Christendom*) had negative effects as well, demonstrated in intolerance and violence directed toward non-Christians.

In modern secular societies, leaders are often reluctant to draw on explicitly religious ideals to motivate citizens to altruism and compassion. But Nussbaum insists that a humanistic investment in those ideals can generate civic devotion and support public compassion. She acknowledges that formal legislation and rational appeals to justice alone do not provide sufficient motivation for civic virtue: "The moral sentiments . . . cannot be simply an embrace of abstract principles presented as such." Deeper motivations for creating and defending a just society must come from the cultivation of emotions. Concretely, this will mean a regular appeal to "symbols, memories, poetry, narrative, or music, which lead the mind toward the principles and in which the principles themselves are at times embedded."

Democratic society thrives as it espouses and defends the conviction that its members merit equal dignity. But the rigors of the law and the dictates of justice are not sufficient to sustain this claim. Emotions of compassion and altruistic care are required to buttress the law's requirements. Nussbaum argues that as the force of religious belief wanes in many modern societies, a stronger secular defense of civic compassion will be required.

Political Emotions and Civic Resilience

Abraham Lincoln's Gettysburg Address was a call for resilience in a time of severe national crisis. He reminded his listeners that the Civil War "is testing whether this nation . . . can long endure." He acknowledged "the great task remaining before us"—a challenge to the nation's resilience—and declared that "we here highly resolve that these dead shall not have died in vain." Lincoln's rhetoric performed the alchemy of turning the civic into the sacred. He repeatedly evoked the sacred notions of "consecration" and of "hallowing" this burial place. Without making explicit reference to Christian beliefs, Lincoln tapped into the national consciousness, which is both civic and spiritual. These presidential words helped make holy this public space.

The virtue of patriotism elicits personal devotion to a widely shared but invisible reality—the common good. This commitment is meant to lead us beyond private and provincial concerns, strengthening our willingness to make sacrifices for the nation's well-being. Stories, symbols, and rituals lie at the source of this civic emotion. Nussbaum notes that "patriotic emotion seeks devotion and allegiance through a colorful story of the nation's past, which points, typically, to a future that still lies in doubt." She cites the French philosopher Ernst Renan's identification of the nation as "a spiritual principle." This spiritual principle involves both "a story of the past, usually a story of adversity and suffering, and then a commitment to the future, a willingness to live together and face adversities for the sake of common goals." She adds, "The two sides are linked, because the story of the past has to tell people what is worth fighting for in the future."

Civic Grieving and Public Art

Citizens of a true democracy will experience both conflict and the need for reconciliation. A dynamic that responds to this aspect of democracy is civic grieving. Nations face the challenge of healing civic wounds. A statue of Abraham Lincoln in Washington, DC, commemorates Lincoln's leadership as president throughout the scourge of the US Civil War. Here he is presented not in the triumphant pose of a hero, but as a leader bent and humbled, himself experiencing the nation's grief at its own self-destruction. The civic art works as "a solemn reminder that the war ought to be seen . . . as a tragedy, a burden we must all shoulder and somehow cope with, and ultimately, put behind us" (Nussbaum).

After the termination of the Vietnam War, Americans again faced the challenge of honoring the nation's suffering in the face of the continuing dispute over the war's legitimacy. The design submitted by a twenty-one-year-old artist of Asian American heritage was selected. Unlike previous displays of heroic soldiers brandishing multiple weapons, Maya Lin designed a stark black stone wall on which were inscribed the names of those who had died in the war. The wall itself was cut into a gentle hillside; visitors approach the site by walking down, as into a crypt. Yet the space itself is not tomblike, but open. The wall of names is constructed of reflective stone, so that visitors closely inspecting the name of a friend or relative see their own faces reflected back. Now identities meld in this moment of memory and sorrow. The site is intensely personal, even as members in the respectful crowd mingle comfortably with one another. Today the memorial serves as a secular sanctuary where even those at odds over the legitimacy of America's involvement in Vietnam can pay tribute, together and in public, for lost loved ones.

New Orleans: Resilience in a Wounded City

At 1:30 p.m. on August 29, 2005, Hurricane Katrina struck the city of New Orleans. During the next two days, the levees protecting the city failed in multiple places; residences and businesses in 80 percent of the city went underwater. Sixteen hundred people died in the metropolitan area, as thousands fled the city, many of them never to return. Schools and hospitals closed; civil services came to a halt. Public officials warned residents and business owners that they might not be able to return for two or three months. The scope of devastation in certain parts of the city made ever returning questionable for many residents. Failures of coordination among local, state, and federal governments exacerbated the collective misery, adding confusion and uncertainty about the city's very future to deep personal anxieties about homes, jobs, neighborhoods, and schools for children. The recovery of the city—its resilience in the face of this catastrophe—was in question.

The profound disruption of local politics and economics resulting from this massive flooding created a temporary vacuum-like state of disorganization that would both provide an opening for and provoke a contest about enhancing the "new New Orleans." In the midst of the civic disarray, a number of reform-minded citizens recognized this crisis as a historic opportunity to rebuild a better city.

Efforts of recovery began with the establishment of the Bring New Orleans Back Commission in October. Within that commission a Government Effectiveness Committee was created with a specific focus on city government. Michael Cowan, a social scientist, joined other members of this committee in addressing aspects of the civic institutions that most desperately awaited change and that would move city government beyond the old "normal," with its layers of corruption and dysfunction, toward a more just and transparent arrangement.

In the state of extreme political and economic disorganization immediately following Katrina, the guiding strategic idea of committee members was that the citizens of New Orleans now had an opportunity not simply to replace what had been lost or damaged in the flood, but rather "to re-create city government for the greater benefit of all by fundamentally reforming its structures, policies and operations" (Cowan).

The Government Effectiveness Committee began its work by reviewing best practices in other cities that had succeeded in preventing waste and fraud. An outside consultant suggested that these other cities had established an Office of Inspector General (OIG), a position that could independently and effectively critique and require reform of corrupt agencies within the city government.

At the same time Michael Cowan organized a citizens' interest group, Common Good, "a group of civil society—non-profit and faith-based—an organization dedicated to seeking consensus across the lines of race, class and religion about rebuilding a New Orleans that would be better for all." Since everything was broken in New Orleans after the hurricane, more issues cried out for attention than one organization could possibly address. The organizing strategy of Common Good was to have a diverse group of religious and civic leaders join government and business leaders in setting priorities and implementing policies aimed at rebuilding the city for the benefit of all. These priorities would be derived from local research and based on best national practices.

The next step was the establishment of a seven-member Ethics Review Board, which would select the person to head the OIG. Common Good discovered in the New Orleans city charter the call for this office, though it had never been operationalized. Common Good members then worked to formulate an amendment to the city charter to authorize guaranteed funding for the OIG, in order to keep it independent of internal political forces.

Cowan, reflecting on the decade of these reform efforts since Katrina, acknowledges that despite continued efforts to "delegitimize the OIG by portraying it as an instrument of whites to check black politicians, the broad sense of public opinion across lines of race, class and geography is that the OIG has become an effective force for interrupting the New Orleans history of waste, fraud and abuse in city government." The OIG has contributed to that perception by creating a level of transparency that for the first time in the city's history allows city administrators, legal authorities, and citizens to hold elected and appointed officials accountable for their stewardship of public resources. The OIG has done what few could have imagined, and none had been able to accomplish before the arrival of the devastating storm. It has created a growing public expectation that waste, fraud, and abuse by elected or appointed officials is much more likely to be exposed, with timely and serious consequences for those who risk misusing public office for personal gain.

Justice at the Gate

Common Good members were also aware that for some citizens, good public institutions are valued as matters of democracy, secular justice, or fiduciary responsibility for public resources. For others, these goals are a religious imperative. The Common Good thus injected into the civic dialogue the Jewish prophetic imperative to establish justice in the city's institutions. About the year 760 BCE the prophet Amos indicted the corrupt tax collectors who controlled the city gates. "I have noted how many are your crimes and how countless your sins. You enemies of the righteous, you taker of bribes, you who subvert in the gate the cause of the needy. . . . Hate evil and love good, and establish justice in the gate" (Amos 5:12–15).

To establish justice in the gate means to create public institutions—including, but not limited to, a criminal justice system—that are lawful, fair, efficient, and effective. For the poorer citizens of the city, the consequences of these reforms mark the difference between enjoying economic opportunity and having to struggle to survive. The consequence for the community as a whole is confidence in public safety. In this biblical appeal for "justice in the gate," Judeo-Christian social values become a second language motivating the work of civic resilience.

Social change is powered by people becoming disturbed about something happening in their social world that should not be allowed or by the absence of elements they see as necessary. Prophetic texts, like the mandate of the biblical prophet Amos to "establish justice in the gate," can empower citizens to seek justice and mercy in their own societies. Prophetic texts motivate religiously oriented actors by reminding them of the ultimate goal of their efforts for social justice and political accountability. These texts announce that humanity shares with God a covenantal responsibility for establishing justice in history.

The capacity for resilience, both for individuals and civic groups, depends on both internal and external resources. Hurricane Katrina's disruption of civic "arrangements" that were corrupt and dysfunctional created an opening for reform-minded citizens who until then had been excluded from participation in these institutions. Already within the city were internal resources of gifted and motivated citizens who were now able to step forward in service of the city's recovery. These citizens were aware that skills beyond their own would be required. With this in mind they sought the advice of an outside consultant, who recommended the establishment of an OIG. The presence and action of this external resource person provided a perspective that had been lacking in the city. Taken together, these new resources tipped the balance of power and set the city on the path to a resilient recovery.

Measuring Civic Resilience: Boston and New Orleans

In the bombing at the marathon in Boston, terrorists struck at the city's pride and exposed its vulnerability. The trauma was intense but brief; the danger was severe but limited. The one civic institution most affected was the long tradition of the marathon, which, while an important element in the city's pride, was peripheral to the city's everyday operation. The immediate response of Boston's citizens rallied the city to heal its injured citizens and wounded pride.

Hurricane Katrina in New Orleans had a wider impact and deeper path of destruction. The scope of devastation included many thousands of citizens, especially the poor. The depth of the disaster, paradoxically, revealed the dysfunction of the city government and opened a path for reform. That reform, following on the actions described above, is now well begun. But the processes of reconstruction have far to go before the term *resilience* can be used with confidence.

Resources

Martha Nussbaum's discussion is found in *Political Emotions* (Cambridge, MA: Harvard University Press, 2013). The discussion here follows her reflections in earlier work, specifically *Hiding from Humanity: Disgust, Shame, and the Law* (Princeton, NJ: Princeton University Press, 2004) and *Upheavals of Thought Thought: The Intelligence of Emotions* (New York: Cambridge University Press, 2001), page 300 and following.

Michael Cowan analyzes the political dynamics taking place in New Orleans after Hurricane Katrina in "Establish Justice in the Gate: Transforming Public Institutions in the Wake of

Natural Disaster" (preliminary report). Also see his essay, "Elbows Together, Hearts Apart: Institutional Reform, Economic Opportunity, and Social Trust in Post-Katrina New Orleans," in *New Orleans under Reconstruction*, ed. C. M. Reese, M. Sorkin, and A. Fontenot (New York: Verso, 2014), 207–27.

Chapter Eight

Resilience in Suffering

Trauma and Tragedy—Healing without Cure

Out of the depths I cry to you,
O Lord. Lord, hear my voice.

—Psalm 130

Pain is bred in the bone, and in sinew, and in nerves. As a universal experience registering physical alarm, pain respects no national boundaries. Suffering is the psyche's response to pain. Here culture plays a significant role. Cultures create stories of courage, scripts of self-sacrifice, and models of resilience to guide us through unavoidable pain and loss. One culture may dictate stoic composure. Another will encourage loud laments or dispense prescription medicine. Through these various strategies, cultures seek to make sense of both discomfort and agony. By investing suffering with meaning and purpose, cultures support personal resilience.

Religious traditions, too, attempt to make sense of suffering. The calm demeanor expressed in a statue of Buddha signals one religious path: by letting go the self-absorption and anxiety that dramatize every loss, we loosen the grip of pain, and our suffering begins to dissolve. The figure of Jesus on the cross tells another story: suffering is part of life's plot. Committing ourselves to mortal persons and to fragile ideals, we are sure to come to grief. But in life we learn that some values are worth suffering to protect, even at the risk of our lives. Suffering, then, cannot be excised from lives of commitment. Both religion and culture attempt to support us in disciplines that temper suffering and build resilience. The biblical tradition includes stories of life and death, of loss and gain, of suffering and redemption. As we are able to find ourselves in these stories, our capacity for resilience expands.

Describing the experiences of her parents and other survivors of the Holocaust, Eva Hoffman offers a clue to understanding suffering. She distinguishes between tragedy and trauma. "Tragic struggle may entail moral agony, but leaves the sense of identity and dignity intact." The suffering of Jesus on the cross was, in this sense, tragic. The experience itself was horrific, but his spirit was not broken.

For Hoffman, the experience of trauma is different. "Trauma is suffering in excess of what the psyche can absorb, a suffering that twists the soul until it can no longer straighten itself out, and so piercingly sharp that it fragments the wholeness of the self." Trauma splinters a person's identity and dignity. The suffering this produces is unbearable, and the grief it generates is life-defeating. In contemporary experience, the suffering of those afflicted with posttraumatic stress disorder (PTSD) reflects a suffering that breaks the spirit and undermines a person's resilience.

Hoffman explores the suffering that her parents endured in the Holocaust, a wound that was handed on to her. Coming to America after having lost most of their extended family during this disaster, her parents brought with them the traumatic grief endured through those experiences. "The legacy they passed on was not a processed, mastered past, but the splintered signs of acute suffering, of grief and loss." Hoffman's task was to transform this inherited trauma into a consciously grieved tragedy. The pain then might be dreadful but not destructive of her personal resilience.

In her reflection Hoffman asks, "How does suffering pass from the unbearable to the bearable?" Her tentative answer is that "suffering shared, suffering respected, is suffering endurable." In the context of sharing and respect, the effort to confront the "forgotten" grief may begin. By bringing suffering into speech, by finding expression in art and ritual, humans become able both to embrace and to relieve their grief.

Speaking of Suffering—Saying No, Saying Yes

Much of the suffering in the world is human-made. Most of humanity's pain and suffering does not "result from the very structure of human life, or from some mysterious necessity of nature. It results from ignorance, greed, malice, and various other forms of badness" (Martha Nussbaum). To such suffering, we must say *no*. This negation begins in the recognition of what the theologian Edward Schillebeeckx calls "experiences of injustice, oppression, and suffering that give rise to protest and the ethical imperative toward active transformation." These negative experiences arouse anger at injustice and hope for something better.

A temptation arises to say *no* to suffering by simply denying its existence. But this silent *no* fails to lessen the distress. Reflecting on the bitter fruit of the Cultural Revolution in his country, a Chinese scholar concludes that when the traumas of those years are not acknowledged but simply endured, they become "sedimented in the body as lack of vigor and sedimented in the mind as cynicism." Those who have suffered may try to forget the horrors of their past sufferings, but their bodies remember; grief that is denied descends into the body, biding its time and resurfacing in the guise of physical symptoms.

Wisdom and resilience are born in discerning the forces that introduce suffering into our lives. To the suffering generated by injustice we are called to say *no*. Yet other suffering—elicited by our affection for a dying friend or by our active support for a controversial cause—invites our *yes*. Here is distress that we would not trade for a disengaged equanimity.

Civic Suffering: Grieving the Civil War

The historian Drew Gilpin Faust has traced the cultural responses to the widespread injury and death that resulted from the Civil War in nineteenth-century America. Prior to this conflict, Americans had associated death with old age— one's death would be experienced at home, surrounded by family members. But this war wrought a profound change. "In the middle of the nineteenth century the United States embarked on a new relationship with death."

Faust analyzes what she calls "the work of death" that emerged in the course of this national conflict. The magnitude of the loss of life on the battle-field demanded reframing. "So much suffering had to have a transcendent purpose." These deaths were celebrated as the ultimate sacrifice, made in support of their young nation's future. The nation moved, practically and symbolically, to create ways to grieve and to honor those who had died.

Lawmakers in the north, for example, established seventy-four national cemeteries as public ceremonial sites to honor the fallen soldiers. This expression of national grieving took on an egalitarian character. "The cemetery at Gettysburg (the site of one of the more horrendous battles) was arranged so that every grave was of equal importance." In this social space the nation testified to the democracy of death.

At a more practical level, society was faced with the challenge of transporting the bodies of thousands of soldiers back home for burial. To meet this challenge, new industries emerged: the mass production of coffins, the medical practice of embalming, and the funeral industry.

Faust concludes: "The war's staggering human cost demanded a new sense of national destiny, one designed to ensure that lives had been sacrificed for appropriately lofty ends." The symbolic gestures associated with national cemeteries helped transform the trauma of the Civil War into a regrettable and tragic event in the nation's history.

Resilience in Suffering: Vulnerability

Suffering, large and small, puts resilience to the test. Pain and the grief it generates can shatter our confidence, question our resolve, and unravel our carefully constructed composure. How will we survive this distress? Suffering forces us to face our vulnerability and lament our losses.

Vulnerability often appears as a liability. Being vulnerable may leave us open to injury and insult, encouraging others to take advantage of our weakness. A soldier's vulnerability can be lethal; any vulnerability a politician shows may lead to her defeat in the next election. We learn to present a strong front to the world, to construct and maintain a well-defended composure. A tradition of stoicism in both our cultural and religious heritage has reinforced this commitment to emotional invulnerability. Marcus Aurelius, Roman emperor and stoic philosopher, judged that "anger is a weakness just as much as grief." Grief was maligned as a *womanish* emotion, a fainthearted refusal to accept the reality of loss. For stoics, both then and now, such emotional vulnerability plays to no advantage.

Yet elsewhere in our culture and in the biblical heritage, vulnerability has been prized as a character strength: the ability to allow ourselves to experience the losses that are unavoidable in any human life. We recognize this vulnerability in the person who, after years of defended denial, finally joins Alcoholics Anonymous; in the vulnerability of the midlife adult now willing to acknowledge the sexual abuse suffered decades ago and until now buried in forgetfulness; in the vulnerability of the soldier returned from the conflict zone who can at last admit the terrors that still stalk his consciousness.

In times of great suffering the need will arise to raise one's voice in sorrow, anger, and accusation. This movement toward expression can mark the moment when silent suffering is transformed. Only gradually do we glimpse the grace of this necessary grieving: grief is a salutary emotion, a necessary virtue that guides us through treacherous times.

Grief stirs us to lamentation, with its cleansing, if scalding, effect. Finally, grief's energy impels us toward the future, uncharted but full of God's promise.

Grief unfolds in expressions of lamentation. Throughout the Hebrew Bible we read again and again of a people's lament. "Since I have lost all taste for life, I will give free rein to my complaints; I shall let my embittered soul speak out" (Job 10:1). "All you who pass this way, look and see: Is there any sorrow like the sorrow that afflicts me, with which Yahweh has struck me on the day of his burning anger?" (Lamentations 1:12). The ancient Jews found comfort in such prayerful complaint. Refusing to harbor their losses in private distress, they turned their suffering into noisy prayer.

Kathleen O'Connor analyzes the paradoxical power of such ritual grieving:

> Lamentation can shred the heart and spawn despair, but, paradoxically, by mirroring pain it can also comfort the afflicted and open the way toward healing. It can affirm the dignity of those who suffer, release their tears, and overcome their experience of abandonment.

O'Conner reflects on "mirroring pain." Our compassionate presence with someone in distress provides a kind of mirror in which they can see, in our company, their own suffering. Our presence may serve as a "reflection" on their sorrow. We provide them opportunity to express their grief, as we offer our companionship in the midst of their pain.

This lamentation may be sounded in unexpected sanctuaries: in the counselor's office, as memories of one's abuse decades earlier are shared; in the circle of veterans retelling stories of horrors seen and committed in battle; over coffee in a café, as a friend hesitantly shares her decision to undertake divorce proceedings. In these significant initiatives, resilience is expressed and reinforced. A courageous person comes through loss and distress, scarred but alive; transformed and stronger than before.

"Healing without Cure"

In the classic Greek drama *Antigone*, the heroine faces a terrible choice: obey the king's command that the body of her disgraced brother remain unburied or honor her family's commitment to undertake the burial rites. Submit to the civil law or follow her moral instincts. Both choices would lead to grief. Reflecting on the audience's response to this drama, Aristotle focused on the emotions of pity and fear. He concluded that in their experience of this moving drama, "all must get a sort of catharsis and be enlightened together with pleasure."

Art, like religion, attempts to take the measure of human suffering. It does not resolve the perennial distress that plagues humanity, but somehow humanizes it. Our pain is rendered more bearable. Thus is the resilience of the human spirit fostered. Martha Nussbaum contends that emotional catharsis, in a theater or in a counseling session or in one's living room, entails a "healing without cure." In this compassionate response to suffering, whether in ourselves or others, we meet the healing power of catharsis. And this capacity for catharsis, Nussbaum comments, "can also give us access to a truer and deeper level of ourselves, to values and commitments that have been concealed beneath defensive ambition or rationalization." This "access to a truer and deeper level of ourselves" offers a firm foundation upon which resilience may be built.

Resources

Drew Gilpin Faust examines the aftermath of the Civil War in *This Republic of Suffering: Death and the American Civil War* (New York: Knopf, 2008). We quote from pages 100, 168, 268.

In his review of Faust's book, "In the Mourning Store" (*New Yorker*, January 21, 2008, 77–81), Adam Gopnik described these social changes as representing "a new cult of memory—a new set of social rituals, some rooted in the Bible, but many intensely secular, the rituals of Republican mourning."

Martha Nussbaum explores "healing without cure" in *The Fragility of Goodness: Luck and Ethics in Greek Tragedy and Philosophy*, rev. ed. (New York: Cambridge University Press, 2001); see 82.

Eva Hoffman's reflections appear in *After Such Knowledge: Memory, History, and the Legacy of the* Holocaust (New York: Perseus Books, 2004), 34 and 54.

The Chinese scholar Ci Jiwei reflects on suffering in *Dialectic of the Chinese Revolution* (Stanford, CA: Stanford University Press, 1994), 96.

Catherine Hilkert comments on Schillebeeckx's discussion of suffering injustice in "Edward Schillebeeckx: Encountering God in a Secular and Suffering World," *Theology Today* 62 (2005): 376–87.

Kathleen O'Connor discusses compassion and "mirroring pain" in *Lamentations: The Tears of the World* (Maryknoll, NY: Orbis Books, 2003). Marcus Aurelius's reflection is found in *The Meditations* (Indianapolis, IN: Bobbs-Merrill, 1963), 11.

Chapter Nine

Resilience at Risk—
The Challenge of Integrity

The Perils of Belonging and
the Virtue of Integrity

*Integrity: honesty, being true to one's word,
willingness to "walk the talk."*

Integrity is a cherished virtue in both the psychological disciplines and the Christian tradition. Erik Erikson defines psychological integrity as a gradually developed capacity to acknowledge all that we are—wounds and all. Other psychologists describe this virtue as including "the ability to embrace and incorporate one's weaknesses and frailties into the whole of the psyche. This process leads to the embodiment of one's genuine self." Here integrity is appreciated as an interior attitude, a character strength, even a personal virtue.

Developmental psychologists also recognize the social dimension of integrity, as a character strength that develops gradually through the exchanges and commitments we forge with one another. It is in league with those who amplify our gifts and tolerate our foibles that we achieve what we could not accomplish alone. Integrating our lives with significant others, we flourish in ways that are unavailable to our private experience.

Personal resilience—the capacity to recover from the insults and injuries that come our way—depends on this dual sense of integrity. Graced with an interior harmony among our own strengths and limits, and securely linked with significant others, we are better equipped to respond with resilience to the setbacks that bruise every life.

The Peril of Belonging: The False Self

Both integrity and resilience are refined in the relationships through which we come to *belong* within our surrounding environment. But such inclusion is a perilous process, whether in our families, our civic lives, or our faith communities. These life-giving settings welcome us and provide the support that underpins our resilience. These groups offer guidelines and cautions intended to safeguard our belonging. Their goal is to help us become "respectable members" of the group. For our part, we are eager to belong, recognizing that our well-being is at stake. And in our search for the consolations of inclusion, we may be tempted to conform to social pressures that, in the end, distance us from our own best instincts. In this way, the *false self* emerges. A young adult, for example, may devote a decade to becoming the doctor or lawyer that her parents ambitioned for her. Only in her thirties does she realize that this achievement has little to do with her own deepest hopes. Here integrity may demand that she acknowledge the disparity, and—even in the face of resistance—chart a new path.

Belonging, with its comforts and demands, is likely to come at an even higher price for those already marginalized by society. Lesbian and gay Christians, struggling to remain connected with their families and welcomed in their communities of faith, may spend years simulating a life that is not true to their self-understanding. Here inclusion comes at the price of pretense. The well-intentioned effort to "fit in" results in the emergence of a false self that compromises personal integrity. Andrew Sullivan has counted the toll that this effort exacts, describing his efforts to keep all relationships superficial to "prevent passion from breaking out." This led, in time, to "a theological austerity [that] became the essential complement to an emotional emptiness."

For transgender persons, whose personal integrity demands resolution of the deeply felt disconnect between their interior sense of gender and their embodied self, the stakes are yet higher. As the result of both societal ignorance and religious prejudices, transgender persons have often felt compelled, sometimes for their own safety, to construct a facade that masks their true gender identity.

The psychologist Diane Ehrensaft describes this dangerous strategy: "The false self is the layer that we build around the true self to protect it from harm and to conform to the expectations of the environment." Further, "it is the congenial face we put on at work . . . the very face that we finally get to take off when we get home, kick up our heels, and let down our hair." The false self is the mask that disguises the fragile identity we dare not entrust to the judgmental arenas of social life.

Jennifer Finney Boylan describes her efforts, as a transgender person, to live under the burden of a false self. "Trying to make the best of things, trying to snap out of it, didn't help, either. As time went on, that burden only grew heavier, and heavier, and heavier." And the price of such make-believe is high: "At every waking moment now, I was plagued by the thought that I was living a lie."

Family and culture, often judging that *difference* signifies *deviance*, may encourage those who are homosexual or transgender to sacrifice personal integrity and settle for a superficial life. Tentative efforts at honest self-disclosure are met with strong resistance. Unfortunately, religious groups often conspire in this refusal to recognize the truth of this person's life. Succumbing to these demands, individuals struggle to play the role that society has assigned them, no matter how deeply at odds with their inner reality. Maintaining this false self, however effective in its disguise, consumes enormous energy.

Thus for many the time comes—and this is the good news—when the masquerade no longer works. Sustaining this deception is simply too costly. And as many attest who have found the strength to discard this false face, the transition toward more genuine self-acceptance is enormously liberating.

The Grace of Crisis

The journey to a more integrated life—with its gift of greater resilience—often begins in crisis. Crisis is frequently portrayed as an unfortunate, even dangerous, intrusion into our lives. But even as crisis threatens a familiar past, it often forecasts a richer future.

In his developmental perspective on human maturing, Erik Erikson offers a more positive interpretation: crisis often arrives as an invitation, however unsettling, to enter a new stage of growth. Erikson explains: "Crisis is used here in a developmental sense to connote not a threat of catastrophe, but a turning point, a crucial period of increased vulnerability and heightened potential."

The crisis of integrity arises in an insistence to trust oneself. Accepting more fully "who I know myself to be," a person moves toward a commitment to integrate this self-awareness with "how I am known to others." This crisis can generate severe anxiety, because so much seems at risk. But paradoxically, this upheaval itself ignites the belief that the transition to a more integrated life is possible. And this hope fuels the determination to embark on the journey, even aware of the perils that lie ahead.

Resilience is put to the test when we face such a crisis. If our interior life is in disarray—when our ideals contradict our customary behavior, or as chronic self-doubt undercuts our decisiveness—we will have trouble marshaling our resources to meet the challenge. In such situations, resilience is diluted or defeated.

The Virtue of Integrity

Psychological integrity names the harmonious state that arises when our words and our actions match, when our behavior is consistent with our interior sense of who we are. The achievement here is wholeness, not perfection. Integrity describes not a complete and well-defended self, but an expanding appreciation of the strengths and weaknesses, the light and shadow, that make us who we are. *Social integrity* names the harmony that arises when we comfortably belong to communities important to us, both benefiting from their support and remaining receptive to their challenges. Our resilience depends on both types of integrity.

Paul chose the metaphor of the physical body to describe the virtue of integrity. In his plea for harmony among the fractious early Christians, Paul insisted: "Now you are the body of Christ and individually members of it" (1 Corinthians 12:27). The body has many components: some parts fit awkwardly in the whole; others are considered inferior or even shameful. The lifelong challenge is integration: bringing the diverse members into harmony and graceful coordination.

The virtue of integrity—harmonizing the diverse parts of ourselves and making peace with our multiplicity—is more than a personal challenge. And Paul offered advice on how this social task may be accomplished: "The members of the body that seem to be weaker are indispensable, and those members of the body that we think less honorable we clothe with greater honor and our less respectable members are treated with greater respect." No member of the body—however self-important—can say of another part, "we do not need you." We are all in this together! "If one member suffers, all suffer together with it; if one member is honored, all rejoice together with it." Here Paul is describing the social body's integrity, the cornerstone of its resilience.

Many Christians today aspire to an institutional integrity that not only harmonizes differences in the community of faith but also strives to overcome the conflicts that continue to divide the larger society. Here the virtue of integrity pivots not on detachment from those who are different, but on attachment to others whose strengths and limits—like our own—can enhance our common life beyond what we as individuals can achieve. The psychologist John Beebe notes the link between such integrity and the virtue of justice: "Integrity involves a willing sensitivity to the needs of the whole, an ethic that combines caring for others in the world with a sense of justice in insisting that others treat us and we treat them as we would like to be treated."

As they move into the later stages of life, many older people report awareness of another sense of personal integration. Looking back over a lifetime, these elders come to an awareness of their life's rich connectedness with the larger story or tradition. Erikson writes of "a sense of comradeship with men and women of distant times and of distant pursuits who have created [traditions] conveying human dignity and love in history."

For Christians this sense of an emotional and spiritual linkage has been expressed in the phrase "the communion of saints." This image does not refer to an ancient gathering of the exceptionally holy, but to an expansive community of believers over many centuries, a collection of saints and sinners who have contributed to and handed on the rich heritage to which our ordinary lives also witness.

The virtue of integrity is finally celebrated in those social arrangements that link us with others—in nurturing children, in crafting human culture, in befriending the poor, in stewarding the resources of the earth we share. As over a lifetime we integrate the gifts, wounds, and complexities of our own lives, we continue to craft the virtue of integrity in our communities: welcoming those we had disregarded, befriending fellow believers we had once marginalized. The virtue of integrity flowers not in an inviolate privacy but in these bracing and sometimes messy engagements that vitally link us with others.

Resources

Erik Erikson explores the developmental sense of crisis in his *Identity, Youth and Crisis* (New York: Norton, 1968), 96. He describes trust and hope in *Insight and Responsibility* (New York: Norton, 1964), 115. He defines the sense of integrity available in old age in *Identity: Youth and Crisis* (New York: Norton, 1968), 139.

Andrew Sullivan's discussion appeared in "Alone Again, Naturally," *New Republic*, November 28, 1994.

L. H. Kalbian emphasizes the societal aspect of the virtue of integrity in her essay "Integrity in Catholic Social Ethics," *Journal of the Society of Christian Ethics* 24, no. 2 (2004): 55–69.

Several essays in *The Psychology of Mature Spirituality*, edited by Polly Young-Eisendrath and Melvin E. Miller (London: Routledge, 2000), explore the virtue of integrity. See especially John Beebe, "The Place of Integrity in Spirituality"; Ruthellen Josselson, "Relationships as a Path to Integrity, Wisdom and Meaning"; and David Rosen and Ellen Crouse, "The Tao of Wisdom."

Chapter Ten

Developing Resilience— Mindfulness and Humor

Redeeming the Time and the Practice of Humor

When we are mindful of what we are doing, we keep our appointment with life.

—Thich Nhat Hanh and Lilian Cheung,
Savor: Mindful Eating, Mindful Life

Resilience appears in our lives as both gift and task. Our immune systems—physiological and psychological—equip us to respond to threat. And this capacity can be enhanced as we practice ordinary behaviors that increase our resilience. Among the practices that build psychological resilience are the exercise of mindfulness and the development of a sense of humor.

Mindfulness is a cultivated ability to pay attention: to observe with compassion the ebb and flow of thoughts and feelings that course through our consciousness. This calm attentiveness, accompanied by self-compassion, frees us to live with greater focus and joy. Mindfulness includes familiarity with the alerts that arise from our muscular frame and nervous system, what might be called the wisdom of the body. Daniel Siegel notes, "Such input from the body forms a vital source of intuition and powerfully influences our reasoning and the way we create meaning in our lives."

Mindfulness is sometimes misinterpreted as a navel-gazing expression of mental narcissism that requires our withdrawal from the messy engagements of real life. But mindfulness is not a neutral or blank presence. "True mindfulness is imbued with warmth, compassion, and interest," the authors of *The Mindful Way through Depression* insist. "The nature of mindfulness is engagement: where there is interest, a natural, unforced attention follows."

Mindfulness supports a developed sensitivity to the range of emotions at play in our hearts. Thus mindfulness serves as an essential element in resilience. Mindfulness supports an internal attunement to our own mood swings and an interpersonal attunement to the emotional states of other people. Both dimensions of attunement support the healing attitude of compassion. The authors of *Savor: Mindful Eating, Mindful Life* emphasize the compassionate side of mindfulness. "When we are mindful, touching deeply the present moment, in the here and now, we gain more understanding, more acceptance, more forgiveness and love of self and others; our aspiration to relieve suffering grows; and we have more chance to touch joy and peace."

Mindfulness—the practiced skill of living in the present—is undone by cultural forces that distract us from our own lives. Chief culprits today are the expectations that we remain always tethered to our mobile devices and subject to the multiple deadlines we have assigned ourselves. As the social critic Kate Murphy notes, "One of the biggest complaints in modern society is being overscheduled, overcommitted, and overextended." Practicing mindfulness, we become more aware of these demands and expectations that leave us distracted, exhausted, and joyless. Being mindful of the flow of duty and desire in our lives, we become more able to *redeem the time* of our lives and to rediscover the humor that lightens our days.

Redeeming the Time

In the King James translation of Paul's letter to the Christians in Ephesus, he urges the community to "redeem the time" (Ephesians 5:16). Here this pastoral leader was not advocating multitasking. Rather he encouraged the community to avoid squandering their precious days in wasteful distractions. Redeeming the time—rescuing ourselves from the overwrought and overscheduled lives we have created for ourselves—continues as a daunting task in our communities today.

What does Paul's advice have to offer us? Our initial response may be defensive: surely we are not to blame! Time surrounds us, pervasive as the air we breathe. And time moves on its own schedule, progresses at its own pace, has its own rhythms . . . most of which are beyond our control. We cannot alter the time of our lives, neither slowing its passage so that we can accomplish more each day nor speeding its movement to help us avoid boredom.

Further intuitions follow. Ultimately time brings bad news. Each passing day announces our aging, with its threatened diminishments of muscle and memory. Time's ultimate destination is our death. Little wonder that we do not always welcome time's passing.

As Christians we are called to redeem the time, but not because time is sinful. Rather, because this aspect of our lives is subject to so many forces that may disrupt or distort our best hopes. Many of us feel caught up in cultural forces that diminish the time available to us each day (leaving us driven or distracted) and empty time of meaning (leaving us without energy or purpose). We redeem time by securing a rhythm in our days that protects us from these extremes. We can develop the daily disciplines that help us be truly *present*—to companions and loved ones and to ourselves— as we recover the balance of duties and desires in our lives.

Redeeming the time, we become more present to our past. Often this allows us to release the memories of guilt and blame that we have been harboring. And we become more present to our future, attentive again to hopes and ideals that we easily lose sight of in our frenetic busyness.

Biblical language offers insight into these efforts to *redeem the time.* Two words are part of the vocabulary of time that plays through Scripture. Paul used the Greek word *kairos* in his discussions of "redeeming the time." This word refers to the experience of time as a season of special insight or oppor- tunity, or perhaps even of heightened vulnerability. Thus at the beginning of Mark's Gospel we read, "The time [*kairos*] is fulfilled and the kingdom of God is at hand" (Mark 1:15). And earlier in the Hebrew Scripture the Psalmist prays, "Cast me now away in the *kairos* of my old age" (Psalm 70:9).

In other biblical passages, time is identified with the more ominous term *chronos*. In some texts, this term points to prolonged periods of illness or obsession. Thus when Jesus is asked to heal someone burdened by illness, he responds "How long a time [*chronos*] has this person been sick?" (John 5:6). In another passage (Mark 9:2) he is asked to attend to a youth who has been demonically possessed for a long period of time (*chronos*). In general English usage today, this more negative nuance survives in the word *chronic*—as in chronic illness or chronic poverty.

In Scripture, as in our own lives, *kairos* identifies periods of decision, insight, and healing. After months of rumination, for example, we sense the opportune moment has arrived for us to make an important choice. Or in the midst of a frenzied day, we catch glimpses of a more peaceful and purposeful way to live . . . and determine to take action to simplify our schedule. These are moments of *kairos*.

Resilience: Finding the Humor

Abraham's aged wife Sarah, learning that
she will conceive a child, laughs out loud.
God wonders what is so funny. "But Sarah said,
'I did not laugh,'" for she was afraid.
God replied, "Oh, you laughed all right."

— Genesis 18:15, our translation

Many experiences in life catch us off guard. Some bring us to tears, but often our response is laughter. Humor arises in our efforts to integrate the incompatible in life. Laughter comes to the rescue when our efforts to understand stumble in the face of complexity, conflict, and incongruity.

Laughter is a multipurpose response, ranging from the child's delightful squeal to the cynic's derision. Basically, laughter relieves tension in the body and promotes relaxation. And laughter is contagious: we laugh most often when we are among others, and laughter often spreads through a group. The psychologist Dacher Keltner comments, "Laughter builds cooperative bonds vital to group living," and "laughter signals appreciation and shared understanding" (*Born to Be Good*).

The Physiology of Humor

Laughter is aerobic exercise: "Our brains use conflict like our muscles use oxygen, or cars use gasoline. Humor empowers us to make decisions and take pleasure in a complex world." The neuroscientist Scott Weems adds, "Humor is also a form of exercise, keeping our minds healthy the same way that physical exertion helps our bodies." Laughter increases vascular activity, thus relieving stiffness by enhancing blood flow throughout the body. Weems argues that laughter "improves immune system function, reduces chemicals associated with joint swelling in arthritis patients, and even helps allergy sufferers combat dermatitis."

The Psychology of Humor

Humor makes virtue out of conflict. Faced with incongruity, we laugh. And humor is intimately linked to surprise. Listening to a joke unfold, we expect one conclusion and are jolted by another. And the jolt is pleasurable. The comedian Steven Wright, with his wry and paradoxical humor, repeatedly demonstrates how jarring the imagination evokes delight. In his comedy routine, for example, Wright casually mentions that he has an extensive collection of beautiful seashells. In the audience, we begin to picture in our imaginations a large room in Wright's house where these splendid specimens are set out as private possessions. Then, after a strategic pause, Wright adds, "I keep them on beaches all around the world." Caught off guard, we laugh as our notion of private possession is wrenched into a more generous view of nature's goods.

Weems comments on this curious link between humor and surprise. "Surprise is important for humor the same way it's important for insight—we take pleasure in being pulled from false assumptions." In humor our mistakes are not embarrassing, but the source of delight. "We enjoy discovering our mistakes because surprise is one of our most valued emotions, as fundamental as happiness or pride." When we are living in a more mindful fashion, we take the time to savor the humorous episodes in our self-serious lives; and, by laughing, we redeem the time.

A Humorless Faith

Laughter has seldom found an honorable place in the Christian heritage. There is little humor in the New Testament; living out one's Christian faith is often presented as a rather sobering task. The core of Augustine's influential theological vision was the conviction that each of us is born in sin, marked with a moral flaw that was handed down to us from Adam and Eve. There is little to laugh about. The theologian Richard Sorabji comments, "The predominant attitude to laughter in much of ancient philosophy, and still more in the Church Fathers, was disapproval."

In his memoir *The Confessions*, Augustine describes his own difficulty with humor. Laughter for him was most often held hostage by shame, arriving in the form of ridicule and derision. He is afraid of being laughed at. At his mother's death, Augustine weeps, even while fearful that others will "laugh him to scorn" for this expression of grief. He even expressed his concern that God will laugh at him for his constant questioning. For Augustine, laughter did not serve as a medium of refreshing shared delight. He seemed unable to appreciate the ways that laughter refreshes and even heals the heart.

Augustine was heir to a biblical tradition that often imaged God as responding to human sinfulness with derision. In Psalm 2 we read, "He who sits in the heavens laughs; the Lord holds his enemies in derision." The prophet Jeremiah complains to God about the ridicule his enemies heap on him: "I have become a laughingstock all day long; everyone mocks me" (Jeremiah 20:7). And just as Augustine feared, laughter survives today as a weapon of ridicule. Aggressive humor invokes sarcasm to insult others. And such biting humor may be aimed at oneself. Weems observes, "Rather than putting others down, self-defeating humorists target themselves, often as a defense mechanism for low self-esteem."

When we view humor as an effort to integrate the incompatible in life, we can recognize how religious faith itself often serves such integration. Sarah, well beyond her childbearing years, is startled to learn that she will conceive a son. How can this be? She can only chuckle. But God hears her laughter and asks the reason. "But Sarah objects, 'I did not laugh,' for she was afraid. And God replied, 'Oh, you laughed all right'" (Genesis 18:15). The core insight of this biblical story is not the limits of Sarah's fertility, but the extravagance of God's ways that overturn our expectations and calculations. All Sarah could do was laugh. Faith brings surprises that upend our earnestness. This should at least provoke a smile.

Humor and Resilience

Humor, fully appreciated as a resource in a mindful life, is an element in resilience: "People who are quick to laugh tend to forget those stressful experiences more quickly than those around them. Humor also helps to ignore the events in our lives that might otherwise cause us pain or harm." Weems adds, "Humorous people may not experience easier lives that those around them, but they often feel as though they do. They're able to block out negative experiences when they're over and move on."

In his study of depression Andrew Solomon discusses humor as a key resource for recovery and resilience. "It takes a certain survivor impulse to keep going through the depression, not to cave in to it. A sense of humor is the best indicator that you will recover; it is often the best indicator that people will love you. Sustain that and you have hope."

Resources

Two insightful resources are Mark Williams, John Teasdale, Zindel Segal, and Jon Kabat-Zinn, The *Mindful Way through Depression* (London: Guilford Press, 2007), and Thich Nhat Hanh and Lilian Cheung, *Savor: Mindful Eating, Mindful Life* (New York: HarperCollins, 2010). The quote at this beginning of this chapter is from *Savor,* 3.

The psychologist Daniel Siegel relates the wisdom of the body to mindfulness in his *Mindsight: The New Science of Personal* Transformation (New York: Random House, 2010), 43 and 29.

For a typical op-ed piece on busyness, see Kate Murphy, "No Time to Think," *New York Times*, Sunday, July 27, 2014.

See Scott Weems's discussion in his *Ha: The Science of When We Laugh and How* (New York: Basic Books, 2014).

Dacher Keltner comments on laughter in *Born to Be Good* (New York: Norton, 2009).

Richard Sorabji reflects on the interpretation of laughter in the early Church in *Emotions and Peace of Mind: From Stoic Agitation to Christian Temptation* (New York: Oxford University Press, 2000).

Andrew Solomon comments on the role of humor in *The Noonday Demon: An Atlas of Depression* (New York: Scribner, 2001).

Chapter Eleven

Practicing Resilience—
Hope and Gratitude

Resources of Hope and Gratitude

If we hope for what we do not see,
we wait for it in patience.

—Paul's Letter to the Romans 8:25

The seedbed of resilience is hope—the expectation, often without warrant, that injury or loss or failure will not utterly defeat us. We hope for what we know we cannot accomplish; and we have hopes for which we cannot account. Roberto Unger identifies this gracious resource as "an uninvited envoy from another world." Not knowing the source of our own hope, we are brought to gratitude. And even as hope and gratitude arise as gifts, we recognize that these responses can be embraced and even practiced.

Hope, abiding in the imagination, announces that "the world could be otherwise." Hope challenges the present, dilutes the potency of the past, and envisions alternate futures. The virtue of hope sees through the present—the demands and duties that fill our days to overflowing. Hope directs our vision beyond the status quo, the received wisdom, the uncontested assumptions about how things ought to be.

And hope alters the past, reminding us we can forgive old injuries and dissolve ancient grievances. Hope proclaims that the future holds more than "more of the same." And the capacity of hope tunes us to promises at play throughout the Scriptures: "Behold, I am doing a new thing; now it breaks forth. Do you not perceive it?" (Isaiah 43:19).

Erik Erikson locates hope in the trust born in the first encounters of infant and parent. In the loving gaze, repeated hugs, and the regular return of the absent parent, the child learns to hope. Through these early interactions a child grows in confidence that the world is trustworthy—here my needs will be recognized, honored, and (often) satisfied. Erikson defines hope as "an enduring belief in the attainability of fervent wishes, in spite of the dark urges and defeats that plague the human experience." For this developmental psychologist, "Hope is both the earliest and the most indispensable virtue inherent in the state of being alive."

As young adults we are likely to identify hope with a mood of optimism and a sense of confidence. Only later, as the disciplines of mid-life have their purifying effect, do we recognize a difference. Optimism is rooted in confidence that we will be successful: with our own skills, backed by stout allies and good companions, how can we fail? Through our middle years this optimism is likely to be bruised as we encounter unjust forces in society and we come up against the limits of our own abilities. Optimism, then, may give way to a more sober judgment, opening us to the richer experience of hope.

Genuine hope often coexists with sadness and disappointment. As illness and accident threaten those we love and social prejudice disrupts the broader community, hope helps us to stay engaged in life. Resilient hope steadies us as we face the inevitability of human suffering. Running deeper than optimism, hope generates the courage and perseverance that can steady us in the face of loss.

Hope sustains us in situations where our own resources—talent or strength or influence—are limited. Hope frees us from the jaded sense that nothing ever really changes. Hope faces us toward what lies ahead, encouraging us that the future may yet yield blessings beyond what we ourselves have been able to produce. And the passion of hope arouses us, generating energy to move toward this promising future.

Victoria McGeer has traced the links between hope and resilience. When obstacles are put in their way, hopeful people become even more determined. They adapt more easily to unexpected circumstances; when one door closes, they look for another to open. In this way, those who hope will often discover untapped resources in the midst of a difficult situation. Fresh alternatives for action begin to emerge, new personal strengths arise. In this way hope strengthens resilience.

Maturing in hope does not demand that the world always satisfy our demands. Hope for a particular outcome may be dashed. But when this disappointment occurs, those who hope are able to explore other possibilities for action. Thus mature hope strengthens commitment. Even when there may be nothing we can do now, our energy is still oriented toward the future. Our interest, our concern, our desires, our passion—these resources continue to be focused on *what might be* . . . gradually transformed into *what can be* . . . even *what will be*. In McGeer's lovely phrase, mature hope leans into the future, ready to act when these actions can do some good.

Learning to Hope Well

The capacity to hope seems to come partly as gift. Psychologists recognize that many factors are involved: family upbringing and social circumstances and perhaps even genetic makeup. How do we expand our capacity for mature hope? A simple answer emerges in the research: we learn to hope well in the company of hopeful people. Mobilizing hope as a resource for social transformation depends to a considerable extent on being in touch with the hopes of others. In the face of the resistant obstacles to change, our resilience often depends on finding a community sustained by mutual support. Such groups maintain a sense of efficacy, of agency, of confidence in their capacity to cope with the difficulties ahead. With these emotionally responsive companions, our own commitments are strengthened as we reinforce each other's hopeful energy.

Especially when our efforts are focused on social transformation or institutional reform, remaining hopeful can depend on being part of a network of hopeful people. Their hopes and our hopes become linked. This mutual support does not mean that we must endorse everything that our partners in social change promote. Sometimes we have to challenge those with whom we share significant commitments: questioning current strategies, urging clearer understanding of our common objectives, proposing different pathways toward our shared goals. But we sustain our hopes best in the company of responsive others.

Honoring Religious Hope

For many involved today in movements of social transformation and institutional reform, our hope is rooted in faith in God. Realizing that we are part of a reality greater than ourselves, we are set free to invest our lives in hopes that will outlive us. Religious hope is not simply a conviction that certain objectives will occur. Rather it is the confidence that, ultimately, God will prevail. This trust in God does not overlook the need for personal courage or the hard work of determined action. But faith supplies an additional support to these ongoing efforts. Thus among religiously sensitive people, hope in God sustains our practical efforts, nurtures our commitment to seek out viable pathways to the future, and motivates our continued action even in the face of delay or defeat.

McGeer identifies hope's contribution to effective social action: "Hope enables us to actively confront, explore, and sometimes patiently work with our limitations, rather than crumpling in the face of their reality." Hope looks toward what lies ahead, anticipating that better possibilities may await. This resource generates courage and perseverance that can steady us in the face of loss. In hope, we remain open to opportunities to renew order and purpose in our life.

The transformative power of hope challenges the finality of the past, as it questions the fatalism of the future. Hope say that the way things are need not be so. This ennobling passion awakens in our imagination more generous visions of a society and self that do not yet exist. Hope supports the promises thorough which we build bridges to this unforeseeable future.

Practicing Gratitude

Gratitude is a "moral memory that binds together those who have exchanged gifts."

—Georg Simmel

Gratitude is an arousal of remembrance. Feeling grateful reminds us of the benefits we have received and of those who are responsible, those who have blessed our life with gifts. Calling to mind previous supportive relationships strengthens us in the face of present danger. And gratitude often reminds us of bonds that still exist, alerting us to the sources of support and comfort that remain available in our current distress. In gratitude, we recognize that we are not alone; from this awareness grows resilience.

Gratitude has broader positive effects as well. The good feelings that gratitude evokes support physiological well-being and adaptive behavior. And gratitude has long been acknowledged as an essential theme in religious experience and spirituality. In this broad context we can identify gratitude as an emotion, a psychological resource, and a spiritual practice.

As an emotion, gratitude registers in our direct experience. This sense of thankfulness seldom arises alone as an isolated emotion. More often our experiences of gratitude include a range of positive feelings—surprise, joy, delight, pleasure. Gratitude alerts us that we have benefited from someone else's actions. We recognize that these actions were intentional, freely offered, and possibly came at some personal cost to the benefactor. This realization leads us to feel connected with the benefactor, perhaps even indebted.

This interpersonal dimension of gratitude is often experienced as positive; we draw closer to those who respond generously to us. Being grateful reminds us that we are not alone. But some of us are wary of indebtedness, with its discomforting hint of dependence. When dependence is threatening, acknowledging gratitude becomes difficult. But recognizing our indebtedness may also move us in deeper appreciation toward experiences of wonder, humility, awe. For many this recognition comes as a religious experience: we are aware of God's continuing provident care even in circumstances that challenge our understanding and acceptance.

Gratitude urges us to act, to give thanks. Being grateful includes a desire to reciprocate in some way, to acknowledge both the gift and the giver. But even in circumstances where we cannot respond directly to the benefactor, a mood of gratitude finds expression in our daily lives. Aware of the ways in which we have been blessed, we respond with greater sensitivity to the needs of those around us. Family members, friends, colleagues, even strangers in distress evoke our interest and active concern. For many people of faith, this psychological dynamic resonates with the gospel imperative "to go and do likewise."

The Virtue of Gratitude

Much contemporary discussion, in both psychological and religious contexts, recognizes gratitude as a virtue. As a virtue, gratitude is a character strength, an abiding sensitivity that makes us more attentive to our lives. We are mindful of both the gifts we have received and the generous intentions of those who provide these benefits. In this way experiencing gratitude alerts us to the wider network of relationships that sustain us. And the virtue of gratitude matures as we embrace our vulnerability. Rather than simply striving to "stand on my own," we recognize that in many circumstances we are not self-sufficient. Yet in gratitude, our neediness is not simply an embarrassment or a threat. We appreciate that we do not always *have to be* self-sufficient; we can be safe in the care and concern of others. Dependence need not dishonor us. Thus gratitude expands our sense of resilience.

For many of us today, gratitude has become part of our spiritual practice. Traditionally, prayer and fasting have been honored as spiritual practices. In contemporary life, the scope of spiritual practice is much broader. Practices are chosen activities that connect us with larger value traditions in ways that form and transform the self. Spiritual practices link us with communities of faith and their enlivening vision of God's presence and action in the world.

Spiritual practices are valued "for their own sake," not just for the utilitarian benefits that may result. As a spiritual practice, gratitude expands mindfulness; we become more aware and more appreciative of humanity's essential interconnectedness. Gratitude leads us to savor, rather than resent, these connections. With this sensitivity, our response to gifts received goes beyond the focused effort to repay our direct benefactors. Gratitude moves us more broadly, toward greater generosity throughout our daily lives.

Gratitude is one of the most widely studied emotions in the positive psychology movement. Research demonstrates that most of us identify gratitude as a pleasant feeling— clearly distinct from a sense of obligation or subservience. And feeling grateful has positive impact in our lives, supporting physical health and physiological well-being and psychological resilience.

Sometimes we resist expressing, or even experiencing, gratitude—concerned that this will place us in a position of indebtedness. But feeling indebted need not be demeaning. Acknowledging those whose interest and actions bless our lives does not diminish us. We can delight in the recognition of their generosity and support. And gratitude can move us toward relationships of mutual concern, as we appreciate how significantly our lives interconnect. Grateful for these shared experiences of care and concern, we experience ourselves as more resilient in the face of life's challenging circumstances. Blessed to be part of this community of the gift, we are deeply grateful. And this experience of gratefulness often generates a sense of awe and reverence, moving us to prayer.

Resources

See Roberto Unger's definition of hope in his *Passion: An Essay on Personality* (New York: Free Press, 1984), esp. 221, 238 and 244.

Erik Erikson relates hope to trust in *Childhood and Society* (New York: Norton, 1950) and *Identity: Youth and Cri-*

sis (New York: Norton, 1968). Victoria McGeer discusses hope in her essay, "The Art of Good Hope," in the *Annals of the American Academy of Politics and Social Science* 592 (March 2004): 100–27.

Georg Simmel defines gratitude in his essay "Faithfulness and Gratitude," in *The Sociology of Georg Simmel*, ed. Kurt Wolff (Nabu Press, 2011).

We offer further reflections on hope and on gratitude as religious emotions in *Nourishing the Spirit: Healing Emotions of Wonder, Joy, Compassion and Hope* (Maryknoll, NY: Orbis Books, 2012). See especially chapter 4, "Anger, Courage and Hope" and chapter 12, "Gratitude and Generosity."

Chapter Twelve

Resilience in Aging
Supporting Lifelong Resilience

O God, from my youth you have taught me and
I still proclaim your wondrous deeds. So even in
old age and gray hairs, O God, do not forsake me.

—Psalm 71:17–18

The voice of the Psalmist twenty-five hundred years ago echoes hopes that enliven our hearts today: "Though you have made me see troubles, many and bitter, you will restore my life again; from the depths of the earth you will again bring me up." Here the Psalmist attests to personal experience of advanced old age. But throughout the centuries during which the biblical psalms were composed, the average life span seldom exceeded thirty years. By the beginning of the twentieth century life expectancy had reached fifty years; today in most industrialized countries this standard approaches eighty years. Living longer, more of us will experience the physical and mental diminishments that often characterize these added decades of life. Living longer, we also experience the opportunity, and the need, to reflect on the meaning of these years.

In *Being Mortal,* the physician Atul Gawande seeks to examine "what it's like to be creatures who age and die, how medicine has changed the experience and how it hasn't, where our ideas about how to deal with our finitude have got the reality wrong." And he adds, "Our reluctance to honestly examine the experience of aging and dying has increased the harm we inflict on people and denied them the basic comforts they most need."

Gawande is unsparing in his account of the details of our decrepitude. As we move from the decades of our sixties and seventies into the advanced season of our eighties and nineties, physical diminishment mounts. The white enamel of our teeth, the hardest substance in the body, begins to wear away; visual lenses lose their elasticity; blood vessels harden, increasing the pressure required to propel blood throughout the body; muscle mass continues to diminish . . . the humbling litany goes on. Evolution has gifted the human body with many backup systems: a second lung, a second kidney, a second gonad. Yet in time even these backups fail. Gawande invites us to face the uncomfortable truth: "There's no escaping the tragedy of life, which is that we are all aging from the day we are born." Yet there is much that can be done to support resilience in the face of this reality.

Bolstering Resilience

For Americans today, growing older is often accompanied by changes in income, residence, and lifestyle. For many there are also experiences of loss—of one's spouse, of cherished friends and companions, of status and vigor and health. Not all these changes need to be, or are, experienced as negative. And the effects of many of the losses of aging can be lessened by personal planning and effective social policy. But change and loss are part of human aging. Diminishment and death are its companions.

With increasing age, more attention must to be given to maintaining health and to compensating for declining physical vigor. Often our social world undergoes major shifts. Many older persons have an experience of retirement, either voluntary or forced, with significant social and financial implications. New roles are adopted (leisured senior citizen, widow, professor emeritus), and former roles must be adapted in a flexible way (after retirement, how do I relate to my spouse? my former work colleagues? my adult children and their families?).

Questions arise about living arrangements. Should we remain in our family home or find a smaller apartment? Should we consider moving to a better climate or stay here where we have roots? With the death of my spouse and other lifelong friends, I am deprived of those whose presence cannot be replaced. Now that I am alone, should I take up residence closer to my married children or strike out on my own? Will I continue to be able to care for my own needs, or should I consider residence in a retirement community? Satisfaction and adjustment in mature age will be influenced by the way in which these age-related issues are resolved.

Psychologists today—along with the personal report of those who have grown old well—alert us that our final decades continue to offer opportunities for psychological and spiritual growth. As more attention is focused on the majority of persons who grow old both gracefully and vigorously, we become aware of the rich possibilities of human maturity that extend across the life span. In their lives we see resilience both required and rewarded.

Resilience as Reframing

Reframing becomes significant as we age. Many of us first experience a shift in perspective as we enter into our middle years. In our forties and fifties, we become newly aware that we have more yesterdays than tomorrows. Earlier we had measured our life's time from our date of birth. Now we find our attention more often turns toward the future, considering the days that remain. This new orientation may ignite a sense of urgency: if we are to make a course correction, in love or work, now is the time. Gawande notes this reorientation in his judgment that as we move through the senior years "a sense of mortality reorders our desires."

The psychologist Laura Carstensen points to other changes in our appreciation of time. "When we were young and healthy, you believe you will live forever . . . and you are willing to delay gratification—to invest years, for example, in gaining skills and resources for a brighter future." Then, in our later years, this orientation shifts: seeing the future as finite and uncertain: "Your focus shifts to the here and now, to everyday pleasures and the people closest to you." As people grow older, "they interact with fewer people and concentrate more on spending time with family and established friends." The reframing includes moving "toward appreciating everyday pleasures and relationships rather than toward achieving, having, and getting."

Life Review

Reframing finds expression in what gerontologists describe as the *life review.* Most of us have witnessed this effort in the elders we know best: an aging aunt or grandparent spends time examining fading photos from decades earlier; senior colleagues at the work site delight in sharing stories about the "good old days."

Moving through our senior years invites reevaluation of both our present and our past. Through much of my adult life I have been identified by the roles and responsibilities and products of my social involvement. I have been spouse, parent, worker, friend, leader, neighbor, citizen. Gradually over the course of my later years these various roles are either removed (my role as worker is removed at retirement; my role as spouse is removed by my partner's death) or significantly changed (family roles change as both parents and adult children age). I must let go some earlier responsibilities and renegotiate my involvement in others.

Reputation, accomplishment, beauty, influence, affection, wealth—throughout my life these have been important sources of my self-esteem. They have helped me know and accept myself. In my deepest moments, though, I have been troubled by their power over me. I have sensed how vulnerable I am to their loss. What if I fail? What if I lose? What if they don't like me? . . . Where will I be then? But surely I must be more than just the sum of the circumstances of my life. Surely there must be other sources from which I draw my sense of identity and worth.

We may have had the opportunity to raise these questions earlier in life, perhaps during a period of significant illness when forced inactivity undermined our confidence. For some a spiritual retreat or long weekend away from work and family may serve as context for these questions. Life events arise as potential rehearsal for the question that unavoidably surfaces in our later years. Beyond the good work and public accomplishments that have given shape to my identity, the question confronts us: What am I worth now?

The recognition that *I am more than what I do* is a critical insight of human maturity. This is a central conviction of every religious tradition as well. Christianity proclaims that the real basis of one's worth lies beyond one's accomplishments, even beyond good works. Ultimately it is God's love that grounds human dignity and the mature sense of self-worth. And God's love is unconditional.

The Christian affirmation of personal worth is relevant not only to the aged, but its power is tested in a particular way in our senior years. To affirm God's love as a source of my worth when my life is going well, where there are several sources of positive evaluation to which I can turn, is itself a movement of grace. The deeper challenge is to affirm the primacy of this love when other sources of value in my life are less available. It is these times that test the power of Christianity to illumine the shadows of human life, to give meaning if not release.

As these questions of personal meaning arise, a range of responses emerge—impulses that have been present before but only in rudimentary form. A new or renewed commitment to self-acceptance struggles against a pervading sense of despair and disgust. Each of these is a possible response to the ambiguous evidence of one's own life. Out of the conflict engendered by these opposing impulses, new strengths of the personality may emerge. Resilience is the fruit of this resolution.

The affirmation of my own life and the acceptance of my aging do not require that I face the present with passive adjustment to whatever happens. Resisting attempts by others to shove me aside, lobbying for more flexible national retirement policies, adhering to a physical regime of good diet and exercise, continuing a schedule of activities and commitments—these efforts too signal our resilient response.

Playing through questions about our identity in our later years are concerns about the fruitfulness of our life. In early adulthood, this question is often answered in the creativity and productivity of our days. In family and at work, we were doing, building, achieving results. As we moved into our middle years, this creativity began to take on a slightly different hue, as caring for what we have created—families and social projects—reinforced our sense of effectiveness. Years later, as our children establish their independent lives and we approach retirement at work, the question arises: What shall my contribution be now? As we mature through creativity and care toward the generosity of letting go, we are introduced to a new stage of fruitfulness.

We may draw consolation from biblical accounts that affirm this new expression of fruitfulness. Moses, having led his people for years until they reached the very border of the land "flowing with milk and honey," sends his people into this new place while he stays behind. Jesus, having recruited and formed his companions, leaves them at his death to determine their own fate. At Pentecost the disciples feel his absence, both painful and generous. Now they must assume responsibility for the future of Jesus' message. But their movement into this leadership role was made possible by the generous absence of the Lord. Similarly, the community of faith is strengthened today by mature leaders who step away from their authoritative positions, leaving room for the next generation to assume responsibility in building up the community of faith.

The Strength of Mature Resilience

At every stage of life, personal resilience supports psychological maturity. Erik Erikson identifies the resilient resource most relevant to our senior years as "the acceptance of one's one and only life cycle and of the people who have become significant to it as something that had to be and that, by necessity, permitted no substitution."

This acceptance moves beyond simple acquiescence toward appreciation and celebration of the unique, though limited, person I have become. I can look back to salute the drama of pain and joy that has brought me to this point. The expected and unexpected happenings of my life are all vitally related to who I am now. If events had been different along the way, I would have become someone different. These differences might have made my life "better" according to some criteria. But I would not be who I am. I can now accept my life at a deeper level. I can affirm that it is good that my life has gone as it has. I can attest to life's meaning because I can affirm the meaning of my own life, even in its ambiguities.

This resilient response to my own life does not eliminate disappointment and regret. Conscious that my life is coming to an end, I recognize that not all hopes have been realized. I know remorse and guilt in the face of what I have done and what I have failed to do. My death will leave much unattended—loved ones will be left behind; new possibilities in the world will go unwitnessed. Without the often difficult effort to come to terms with my life's disappointments, my self-acceptance remains fragile and unconvincing—even to myself.

The Virtue of Wisdom

When resilience supports such personal integrity, when the impulse toward meaning resists the dynamics of regret and despair, the older person displays the essential strength of character that is wisdom.

Wisdom is manifest in a variety of forms—as ripened wit, as accumulated experience, as mature judgment. Those who we call wise display an inclusive understanding, a widened empathy, a broadened appreciation of diversity and pluralism. Some older persons give expression to this wisdom in the formulation of a personal philosophy of life to which they can give eloquent testimony. In others this wisdom remains implicit, displayed in their attitudes and actions more than in their words. We are aware of it only in the quiet reassurance we feel when we are with them.

Wisdom can transcend, to some degree, the inevitable diminishments of old age. This strength enables the aged person to maintain confidence in the integrity of personal experience in the face of the decline of bodily and mental functions that can mark the last years. Old age brings real diminishments, especially in its final phases. Much can be done to delay and to moderate the negative effects of growing older and being old. But there are real losses in growing old, particularly in the later years of old-old age.

Decreasing physical vigor is sometimes accompanied by ill health. The loss of loved ones through death narrows the circle of true intimates, those with whom one shares not only the present but the richness of a common past. Physical, financial, and social factors may combine to undermine my independent ability to care for my own life. The recognition and acceptance of an increasing dependence can be the most difficult task of our final years.

The real deprivations of old age, and the feelings of anger and regret they evoke, can overwhelm the older person. If these are not opposed and ultimately (or at least periodically) overcome by a sense of the wholeness of one's life, by an affirmation of its meaning, then negativity can become the dominant tone, the prevailing mood of one's final years.

Here our resources of maturity are most keenly tested and the strength of resilience most required. To be sure, the need for personal confirmation continues throughout life. But the mature resources of resilience bring increased capacity to stand free, apart from this confirmation. Such transcendence may be elusive, experienced more in a moment of intuition than as a constant conviction. But this depth of wisdom is possible to the human soul. In the moments of this profound awareness my aging, my diminishment—even my death—may be transformed.

Resilience in my senior years supports an appreciation that my life, in its particularity and peculiarity, has been good. My lifestyle has contributed to who I am today and to the meaning my life has had over its course. It is one of the ways in which human life can be lived meaningfully. In this deep acceptance of my particular life's journey, I can experience an expansion beyond the narrow focus of self-concern. I can savor the awareness that I am one with humankind, with all creation.

In our most senior years we can relish the relationships of family and faith and civic community that have given shape to our belonging. Not to feel strongly linked to anyone or anything as we age is to court a loneliness that is not far from despair. We belong to our past, scars and all. And, in hope, we belong to the future—a season to be crafted by the next generation, to whom we have bequeathed the values that mean the most to us. Our awareness of belonging includes a sense of prevailing. The ideals and goals that have inspired us will endure, even beyond our lives. These values will outlive us, and in this we can rejoice. We celebrate this solidarity in a variety of ways in the Christian community. In the Feast of All Souls celebrated in early November, we recall those who have gone before us, who were strengthened by values that continue to guide the community of faith even today. In the remembrance of "the communion of saints" included in each Sunday's liturgy, we likewise join ourselves to this rich spiritual heritage of saints and sinners. Here, too, we affirm our hope in the resilience of the community of faith.

Resources

Atul Gawande provides a valuable discussion of aging and death in his *Being Mortal: Medicine and What Matters in the End* (New York: Henry Holt, 2014).

Laura Carstensen and her colleagues report evidence of positive emotions among elders in "Emotional Experience Improves with Aging: Evidence Based on Over Ten Years of Experience Sampling," *Psychology and Aging* 26, no. 1 (2011): 21–33.

George Vaillant focuses on men's experience of aging in "Successful Aging and Psychosocial Well-Being," which appears as a chapter in *Older Men's Lives*, edited by Edward Thompson (Thousand Oaks, CA: Sage Publications, 1990).

In *Spiritual Resiliency and Aging: Hope, Relationality, and the Creative Self* (Amityville, NY: Baywood, 2012) Janet Ramsey and Rosemary Blieszner review theoretical perspectives and research findings that demonstrate the significance of spiritual resources—both personal and communal—in the movement through the senior years.

Portions of this chapter are adapted from "To Grow Old among Christians," which appeared in our earlier book *Christian Life Patterns: The Psychological Challenges and Religious Invitations of Adult Life* (New York: Crossroad, 1992).

Bibliography

American Psychological Association. "The Road to Resilience." www.helping.apa.org.

Armstrong, Karen. *The Great Transformation: The Beginning of Our Religious Traditions*. New York: Knopf, 2006.

———. *A Short History of Myth*. New York: Canongate, 2005.

Beebe, John. "The Place of Integrity in Spirituality." In *The Psychology of Mature Spirituality: Integrity, Wisdom, Transcendence,* edited by Polly Young-Eisendrath and Melvin E. Miller. London: Routledge, 2000.

Brooks, Arthur. "The Downside of Inciting Envy." *New York Times*, Sunday, March 2, 2014.

———. "The Father's Example," *New York Times*, Saturday, June 14, 2014.

Cacioppo, John, Harry Reis, and Alex Zautra. "Social Resilience: The Value of Social Fitness with an Application to the Military." *American Psychologist* 66 (January, 2011): 43–51, esp. 44.

Carey, Benedict. "On Road to Recovery, Past Adversity Provides a Map." *New York Times*, Tuesday, January 4, 2011, D5.

Carstensen, Laura. "Emotional Experience Improves with Aging: Evidence Based on Over Ten Years of Experience Sampling." *Psychology and Aging* 26, no. 1 (2011): 21–33.

Ci Jiwei. *Dialectic of the Chinese Revolution*. Stanford, CA: Stanford University Press, 1994.

Connelly, William. *A World of Becoming*. Durham, NC: Duke University Press, 2001.

Cottingham, John. *The Spiritual Dimension: Religion, Philosophy, and Human Value*. New York: Cambridge University Press, 2005.

Cowan, Michael. "Elbows Together, Hearts Apart: Institutional Reform, Economic Opportunity, and Social Trust in Post-Katrina New Orleans." In *New Orleans under Reconstruction,* edited by C. M. Reese, M. Sorkin, and A. Fontenot, 207–27. Brooklyn: Verso, 2014.

———. "Establish Justice in the Gate: Transforming Public Institutions in the Wake of Natural Disaster." Preliminary report shared with authors.

Davidson, Richard J., with Sharon Begley. *The Emotional Life of Your Brain*. New York: Penguin, 2012.

Dreazen, Yochi. *The Invisible Front*. New York: Crown, 2014.

Emmons, Robert. *The Psychology of Ultimate Concern*. New York: Guilford Press, 1999.

Epstein, Mark. *Open to Desire*. New York: Penguin, 2005.

―――. *Thoughts without a Thinker.* New York: Basic Books, 1995.

Erikson, Erik H. *Childhood and Society.* New York: Norton, 1950.

―――. *Identity: Youth and Crisis.* New York: Norton, 1968.

Faust, Drew Gilpin. *This Republic of Suffering: Death and the American Civil War.* New York: Knopf, 2008.

Filkins, Dexter. "The Long Road Home." *New York Times,* Sunday, March 9, 2014.

Finkel, David. *Thank You for Your Service.* New York: Farrar, Straus and Giroux, 2013.

Folkman, Susan. *Resilience: The Meanings, Methods, and Measurement.* New York: Oxford University Press, 2010.

―――, ed. *The Oxford Handbook of Stress, Health, and Coping.* New York: Oxford University Press, 2010.

Frederickson, Barbara. *Positivity: The Role of Positive Emotions in Positive Psychology.* New York: Crown, 2009.

Gawande, Atul. *Being Mortal: Medicine and What Matters in the End.* New York: Henry Holt, 2014.

Geertz, Clifford. *Available Light: Anthropological Reflections on Philosophical Topics.* Princeton, NJ: Princeton University Press, 2008.

Giffords, Gabrielle. "The Lessons of Physical Therapy." *New York Times*, January 8, 2014.

Giffords, Gabrielle, and Mark Kelly. *Enough: Our Fight to Keep America Safe from Gun Violence.* New York: Scribner, 2014.

Gopnik, Adam. "In the Mourning Store." *New Yorker*, January 21, 2008, 77–81.

Gritemeyer, Tobias. "Civil Courage." *Journal of Positive Psychology* 2 (2007): 115–19.

Guntzel, Jeff Severns. "Beyond PTSD to 'Moral Injury': On Jonathan Shay's Notion of 'Moral Injury.'" On Krista Tippett's website, www.onbeing.org.

Hanh, Thich Nhat, and Lilian Cheung. *Savor: Mindful Eating, Mindful Life.* New York: HarperCollins, 2010.

Harrington, Anne. *The Cure within: A History of Mind-Body Medicine.* New York: Norton, 2008.

Higgins, Gina O'Connell. *Resilient Adults: Overcoming a Cruel Past.* San Francisco: Jossey-Bass, 1994.

Hilkert, Catherine. "Edward Schillebeeckx: Encountering God in a Secular and Suffering World." *Theology Today* 62 (2005): 376–87.

Hoffman, Eva. *After Such Knowledge: Memory, History, and the Legacy of the Holocaust.* New York: Perseus Books, 2004.

Janeway, Elizabeth. *Powers of the Weak.* New York: Knopf, 1981.

Josselson, Ruthellen. "Relationship as a Path to Integrity, Wisdom, and Meaning." In *The Psychology of Mature Spirituality: Integrity, Wisdom, Transcendence,* edited by Polly Young-Eisendrath and Melvin E. Miller. London: Routledge, 2000.

Kalbian, L. H. "Integrity in Catholic Social Ethics." *Journal of the Society of Christian Ethics* 24, no. 2 (2004): 55–69.

Kegan, Robert. *The Evolving Self.* Cambridge, MA: Harvard University Press, 1982.

Keltner, Dacher. *Born to Be Good.* New York: Norton, 2009.

Khoshaba, Deborah. "Power." www.HardinessInstitute.com.

Klay, Phil. "After War: A Failure of the Imagination." *New York Times,* Sunday, February 9, 2014.

———. *Redeployment.* New York: Penguin, 2014.

Kornfield, Jack. "Stopping the War." Excerpt from *A Path with Heart:* On the Young Medic's Experience of War and Self-compassion. www.yin4men.com.

Kristof, Nicholas, and Sheryl WuDunn. *A History of Mind-Body Medicine.* New York: Norton, 2008.

Leunig, Michael. *Curly Pajama Letters.* Melbourne: Viking Australia, 2006.

MacIntyre, Alasdair. *After Virtue: A Study in Moral Theory.* Notre Dame, IN: University of Notre Dame Press. 1981.

Mandela, Nelson. *Conversations with Myself.* New York: Farrar, Straus and Giroux, 2010.

———. *Long Walk to Freedom, The Autobiography of Nelson Mandela.* New York: Little, Brown, 1994.

Marcus Aurelius. *The Meditations.* Indianapolis, IN: Bobbs-Merrill, 1963.

McGeer, Victoria. "The Art of Good Hope." *Annals of the American Academy of Politics and Social Science,* 592 (March 2004): 100–27.

Murphy, Kate. "No Time to Think." *New York Times,* July 27, 2014.

Neiman, Susan. *Evil in Modern Thought: An Alternative History of Philosophy.* Princeton, NJ: Princeton University Press, 2002.

———. *Moral Clarity: A Guide for Grown-up Idealists.* New York: Harcourt, 2008.

Nouwen, Henri. *Life of the Beloved.* New York: Crossroad, 1993.

Nussbaum, Martha. *The Fragility of Goodness: Luck and Ethics in Greek Tragedy and Philosophy*. Rev. ed. New York: Cambridge University Press, 2001.

———. *Hiding from Humanity: Disgust, Shame, and the Law*. Princeton, NJ: Princeton University Press, 2004.

———. *Political Emotions*. Cambridge, MA: Harvard University Press, 2013.

———. *Upheavals of Thought: The Intelligence of Emotions*. New York: Cambridge University Press, 2001.

O'Connor, Kathleen. *Lamentations: The Tears of the World*. Maryknoll, NY: Orbis Books, 2003.

Ong, Anthony, C. S. Bergerman, and Steven M. Baker. "Resilience Comes of Age: Defining Features in Late Adulthood." *Journal of Personality* 6 (December 2009): 1777–1804.

Packer, George. "Home Fires." *New Yorker*, April 7, 2014.

Pargament, Kenneth. *The Psychology of Religion and Coping: Theory, Research, Practice*. New York: Guilford Press, 1997.

Pieper, Josef. *The Four Cardinal Virtues*. South Bend, IN: University of Notre Dame Press, 1966.

Povoledo, Elisabetta. "Pope Francis Beatifies an Earlier Reformer, Paul VI." *New York Times*, Monday, October 20, 2014.

Powers, Kevin. *Letters Composed during a Lull in the Fighting: Poems*. New York: Little Brown, 2014.

Ramsey, Janet, and Rosemary Blieszner. *Spiritual Resiliency and Aging: Hope, Relationality, and the Creative Self*. Amityville, NY: Baywood, 2012.

Reich, Alex, and John Zautra. *The Psychology of Everyday Life*. New York: Oxford University Press, 2010.

Rodriguez, Richard. *Darling: A Spiritual Autobiography.* New York: Viking, 2013.

Rogers, Carl. *Personal Power: Inner Strength and Its Revolutionary Impact.* New York: Delacourt, 1978.

Rosen, David, and Ellen Crouse. "The Tao of Wisdom." In *The Psychology of Mature Spirituality: Integrity, Wisdom, Transcendence,* edited by Polly Young-Eisendrath and Melvin E. Miller. London: Routledge, 2000.

Schama, Simon. *The Story of the Jews.* New York: HarperCollins, 2013.

Scheler, Max. "Negative Feelings and the Destruction of Values: *Ressentiment.*" In *Max Scheler on Feeling, Knowing, and Valuing,* edited by Harold Bershady. Chicago: University of Chicago Press, 1992.

Schmitt, Mark. *The Age of Austerity: How Scarcity Will Remake American Politics.* New York: Doubleday, 2012.

———. "Within Limits." *New York Times,* Sunday, January 22, 2012, 16.

Sennett, Richard. *Authority.* New York: Vintage Books, 1981.

Shanker, Thom, and Richard Oppel. "War's Elite Tough Guys, Hesitant to Seek Healing." *New York Times,* Friday, June 6, 2014.

Shay, Jonathan. *Achilles in Vietnam.* New York: Atheneum, 1994.

———. *Odysseus in America: Combat Trauma and the Tales of Homecoming.* New York: Scribner, 2003.

Siegel, Daniel. *Mindsight: The New Science of Personal Transformation.* New York: Random House, 2010.

Simmel, Georg. "Faithfulness and Gratitude." In *The Sociology of Georg Simmel,* edited by Kurt Wolff. Nabu Press, 2011.

Smith, Bruce W., J. Alexis Ortiz, Kathryn T. Wiggins, Jennifer F. Bernard, and Jeanne Dalen. "Spirituality, Resilience, and Positive Emotions." In *Oxford Handbook of Psychology and Spirituality*, edited by Lisa J. Miller, 437–54. New York: Oxford University Press, 2012.

Smith, Glenn. "The Dangers of Political Resentment." September 4, 2011. shadowproof.com.

Smith, Jada. "Using Flags to Focus on Veteran Suicides." *New York Times*, Friday, March 28, 2014.

Solomon, Andrew. *Far from the Tree: Parents, Children, and the Search for Identity*. New York: Scribner, 2012.

———. *The Noonday Demon: An Atlas of Depression*. New York: Scribner, 2001.

Sorabji, Richard. *Emotions and Peace of Mind: From Stoic Agitation to Christian Temptation*. New York: Oxford University Press, 2000.

Southwick, Steven, and Dennis Charney. *Resilience: The Science of Mastering Life's Greatest Challenges*. New York: Cambridge University Press, 2012.

Sullivan, Andrew. "Alone Again, Naturally," *New Republic*, November 28, 1994.

Taylor, Charles. *A Secular Age*. Cambridge, MA: Harvard University Press, 2007.

Turner, Brian. *My Life in a Foreign Country: A Memoir*. London: Jonathan Cape, 2014.

Unger, Roberto. *Passion: An Essay on Personality*. New York: Free Press, 1984.

———. *The Self Awakened*. Cambridge, MA: Harvard University Press, 2007.

Vaillant, George. "Positive Emotions, Spirituality, and the Practice of Psychiatry." *Mental Health, Spirituality and the Practice of Psychiatry* 6 (2008): 48–62.

———. *Spiritual Evolution: A Scientific Defense of Faith.* New York: Doubleday, 2009.

———. "Successful Aging and Psychological Well-Being." In *Older Men's Lives,* edited by Edward Thompson, 22–41. Thousand Oaks, CA: Sage Publications, 1990.

Weems, Scott. *Ha: The Science of When We Laugh and How.* New York: Basic Books, 2014.

Whitehead, Evelyn Eaton, and James D. Whitehead. *Christian Life Patterns.* New York: Crossroad, 1992.

———. *The Emerging Laity: Returning Leadership to the Community of Faith.* New York: Doubleday Religious Publishing Group, 1986.

———. *Nourishing the Spirit: The Healing Emotions of Wonder, Joy, Compassion and Hope.* Maryknoll, NY: Orbis Books, 2012.

———. *Seasons of Strength: New Visions of Adult Christian Maturing.* Lincoln, NE: I-Universe, 2003.

Williams, Mark, John Teasdale, Zindel Segal, and Jon Kabat-Zinn. *The Mindful Way through Depression.* London: Guilford Press, 2007.

Winnicott, D. W. *Home Is Where We Start From.* New York: Norton, 1986.

Wright, Steven. "I have the world's largest seashell collection." www.brainyquote.com.

Yearley, Lee H. *Mencius and Aquinas: Theories of Virtue and Conceptions of Courage.* Albany: State University of New York Press, 1990.

Yeung, Douglas, and Margaret T. Martin. "Spiritual Fitness and Resilience: A Review of Relevant Constructs, Measures, and Links to Well-Being," RAND Project AIR FORCE Series on Resiliency, 2014.

Yousafzai, Malala, with Christina Lamb. *I Am Malala*. New York: Little, Brown, 2013.

Zautra, Alex J. and John W. Reich. "Resilience: The Meanings, Methods, and Measures of a Fundamental Characteristic of Human Adaptation." In *The Oxford Handbook of Stress, Health, and Coping*, edited by Susan Folkman. New York: Oxford University Press, 2011.

Index